NATURAL RESOURCES, GROWTH, AND DEVELOPMENT

NATURAL RESOURCES, GROWTH, AND DEVELOPMENT

Economics, Ecology, and Resource-Scarcity

Clement A. Tisdell

New York
Westport, Connecticut
London

Library of Congress Cataloging-in-Publication Data

Tisdell, C. A. (Clement Allan)
    Natural resources, growth, and development : economics, ecology
and resource-scarcity / Clement A. Tisdell.
        p. cm.
    Includes bibliographical references.
    ISBN 0-275-93479-9 (alk. paper)
    1. Economic development—Environmental aspects. 2. Natural
resources—Management. 3. Developing countries—Economic policy.
4. Natural resources—Developing countries—Management. I. Title.
HD75.6.T565 1990
333.7'09172'4—dc20   90-42118

Library of Congress Catalog Card Number: 90-42118
ISBN: 0-275-93479-9

First published in 1990

Praeger Publishers, One Madison Avenue, New York, NY 10010
An imprint of Greenwood Publishing Group, Inc.

Printed in the United States of America

The paper used in this book complies with the
Permanent Paper Standard issued by the National
Information Standards Organization (Z39.48-1984).

10 9 8 7 6 5 4 3 2 1

Copyright Acknowledgements

Extracts from the author's articles, "Sustainable Economic Growth Production and Development: An Overview of Concepts and Changing Views," *Indian Journal of Quantitative Economics* 4, no. 1 (1988): 73–86; and "Rural-Urban Migration and Labour Allocation: Labour Surplus Models and Alternatives," *Indian Journal of Quantitative Economics* 4, no. 2 (1988); are reprinted courtesy of the *Indian Journal of Quantitative Economics*.

Extracts from the author's articles, "Economics and the Debate about Preservation of Species, Crop Varieties and Genetic Diversity," *Ecological Economics* 2 (1990), reprinted courtesy of Elsevier Science Publishers, Physical Sciences & Engineering Div., Amsterdam, Netherlands.

Extracts from the author's article, "Environmental Conservation: Economics, Ecology and Ethics," *Environmental Conservation* (Summer Issue) (1989): 107–112, 162, are reprinted courtesy of The Foundation for Environmental Conservation, Geneva, Switzerland.

Contents

Illustrations

TABLES

Preface

In the past there has been a tendency to consider economics and ecology independently in examining economic growth and development. But such an approach is no longer tenable, as will be apparent from this book. To an ever-increasing extent economic activity, growth, and development determine the ecological environment of the globe, and this, in turn, places limits on the sustainability of economic activities. Thus economic change, growth, and development need to be assessed in terms of ecological economics. The approach taken in this book to consider issues in economic development combines economics and ecology, the approach recommended in the *World Conservation Strategy* (IUCN, 1980) and by the World Commission on Environment and Development (1987) established by the General Assembly of the United Nations. This, however, is not to say that I agree with all the policy recommendations contained in the *World Conservation Strategy* and in *Our Common Future* (World Commission on Environment and Development, 1987).

In this book I have tried to examine traditional issues in economic development within their wider environmental context, as well as to cover issues not traditionally addressed by economists. Thus I hope this book will be of interest both to readers interested in conventional economic theory as well as those wishing to focus on less conventional issues. However, the issues discussed here should be of interest not only to economists and ecologists but to everyone concerned about our economic and global environmental future.

This book grew out of a series of invited lectures I gave in New Zealand as William Evans Visiting Professor in the Department of Economics, University of Otago, Dunedin. On my return to Australia, the notes used for these lectures and seminars were expanded and revised at the University of Newcastle and at the University of Queensland. I wish to thank all these institutions for their assistance.

The original lectures and seminars were presented to groups with diverse interests. Depending upon the presentation, participants included economists, biologists, geographers, entomologists, environmental scientists, agricultural scientists, undergraduate economics students, and members of the general public. The genesis of various chapters is as follows: Chapter 2 is based on an open lecture given at the University of Otago; Chapter 3 arose from a lecture to a development economics class at the same university; Chapter 4 is derived from a lecture given to an energy economics class, also at the University of Otago. Chapter 5 incorporates material presented to an interdepartmental seminar arranged by the Department of Economics at Waikato University and given further exposure in an invited lecture at Avondale College, New South Wales. Chapter 6 was developed from a paper presented at an interdepartmental seminar arranged by the Department of Agricultural Economics at Lincoln College; the material in Chapter 7 was given exposure at a seminar arranged by the Yellow-eyed Penguin Trust at Otago Museum; Chapter 8 on the biological control of pests is based on a seminar presentation at Auckland University arranged by the Department of Economics and attended by economists, environmental scientists, and members of the Division of Entomology of the Department of Scientific and Industrial Research. Some of the material in Chapter 9 was presented to development economics classes at Lincoln College and at the University of Otago, and that in Chapter 10 arises from a seminar paper read and discussed in economics departments at the University of Canterbury and at the University of Otago. I wish to thank the individuals and institutions that invited me to present papers and those who provided me with feedback on them.

Many individuals provided support for this book in one way or another, including making me feel at home in New Zealand. They include Priyatosh Maitra, who has commented in depth on material contained in a number of chapters, his family, Moira and John Parker, who introduced me to the yellow-eyed penguin problem, John Ward, Steve Jones, Rodney St. Hill, David Giles, Ajit Dasgupta, Ross Cullen, Mike Cooper, the McLeods, and the Moores. The late Iain Lonie encouraged me to write my notes up in a form suitable for a book, and Professor David McKee of Kent State University, Ohio, kindly suggested Praeger Publishers to me as possible publishers. Sally Duncan provided typing assistance in New Zealand, Kath Kirby and Jenny Hargrave typed the first draft of the manuscript at the University of Newcastle, and Deborah Ford typed the final draft at the University of Queensland. Many thanks to them all. Thanks also to my wife Mariel, and children Ann-Marie and Christopher, for being patient and supportive once again.

NATURAL RESOURCES, GROWTH, AND DEVELOPMENT

1

Introduction to Resource-Scarcity, Growth, and Development

RESOURCE SCARCITY AND ECONOMIC GROWTH

The basic economic problem is considered to be how to manage or administer resources so as to minimize scarcity, that is, to minimize the "gap" between individuals' demand for commodities and the available supply of these (Tisdell, 1972, chapter 1; Robbins, 1932). The scarcity problem explains the interest of economists in the efficiency of alternative social mechanisms for resource allocation and their interest in economic growth and in development. A scarcity problem is generally agreed to exist because available resources are insufficient to satisfy fully the wants of everyone, and this situation is believed to continue to persist in the foreseeable future. Even though calls have been made for human beings, especially those with high incomes, to reduce their levels of consumption and demand on resources (Daly, 1980), on the whole such exhortations appear to have fallen on deaf ears. However, even at lower levels of aggregate demand on resources, problems in economizing would still remain.

Despite widespread agreement among economists that scarcity is and will continue to be an important problem, sharp differences of opinion exist about whether it will become a more serious problem, especially as a result of natural resource depletion and environmental deterioration.

Optimists argue that, particularly as a result of technological progress, scarcity of natural resources is likely to become a diminished constraint on the fulfilment of human wants. Natural resource availability and environmental factors are not seen as providing significant limits to economic growth. Indeed, the most optimistic thinkers see economic growth as a positive means to reduce scarcity permanently through the accumulation of capital and knowledge and other effects. Some growth optimists see global advantages through greater economies of scale and argue that economic growth results in a faster rate of technological progress. Optimistic views about the possibility of continuing economic growth (and the view that it is desirable) have dominated economic thought for the last 100 years or so.

However, rosy views about prospects for continuing economic growth are not universal, and serious doubts have been raised about the desirability of continuing economic growth. Criticism of the optimistic economic growth position, which had already gained ground in the 1960s, became more intense in the 1970s as energy prices began to rise. The view was put that economic growth, far from being a cure for the scarcity problem, will exacerbate the problem in the future. A number of writers forecast that as a result of continuing economic growth serious resource shortages were imminent and that a scenario of economic crisis and catastrophe for mankind was possible in the foreseeable future. One of the remedies suggested is to reduce the level of economic production or at least halt its growth via constraints on population increase and on the level of consumption per head.

Growth pessimists argue that, contrary to the claim of the optimists, economic growth can be expected to intensify resource-scarcity. Thus the solution is seen as a problem. This is seen to be so for one or more of the following reasons: (1) The more rapid economic growth becomes, the faster is the depletion of non-renewable resources. (2) Economic growth and production results in waste materials and pollution as a by-product, and this may damage natural resources and reduce their productivity and economic value. (3) Higher rates of economic growth and production can be expected to result in the extinction of a large number of species of living things and thus will reduce the productivity of natural resources, if not immediately, then eventually. In addition, growth pessimists argue that there is no reason to suppose that technological progress will continue to more than counteract the forces making for greater scarcity, even though it has been able to do this in the past. In fact, the pessimists dismiss the possibility that technological progress will be sufficient to more than offset the forces making for greater scarcity of commodities.

Of course, not all views about the relationship between economic growth and resource-scarcity are black and white, in the sense of being absolutely optimistic or absolutely pessimistic. A third view worth considering is that as economic growth proceeds, the risks of resource-scarcity increase.

However, even in relation to rising risks of resource-scarcity or economic disaster due to resource-depletion, several events are possible. These include the following:

1. The probability of resource-disaster may rise.

2. The penalty of resource-exhaustion may increase.

3. Large or catastrophic losses may become possible even though the expected probability of resource disaster does not rise greatly. Large global losses with low probability may become possible as economic growth proceeds.

4. The dispersion of production possibilities, that is, the uncertainty of possibilities, may become greater as growth proceeds.

These possibilities are not necessarily incompatible; it is possible to hold some without necessarily accepting all the others, or to accept them all as a prediction of future consequences of continuing economic growth. But the adoption of one or more of the above propositions can be expected to make us more cautious about advocating economic growth as a means for reducing resource-scarcity and may lead us to recommend that economic growth be constrained or made to satisfy particular conditions. Any one of the above possibilities may be sufficient for risk-avoiders to reject economic growth as an acceptable policy for reducing resource-scarcity. Those rejecting such a policy cannot all be classified as pathological pessimists; they may be acting rationally—that is in accordance with their objectives and reasonable perceptions of reality.

Common and Pearce (1973) have argued that risk avoidance should result in economic growth not being favored or persisted with as a policy intended to reduce resource-scarcity. Lecomber (1979) has, however, criticized this view, suggesting that the risks of reduced scarcity if economic growth does not continue may be greater than if it does. While Lecomber (ibid.) accepts the proposition that there is great uncertainty about the eventual effects of continuing economic growth, he is unclear about whether the growth option should be rejected, especially since continuing economic growth may be associated with greater technological progress.

Whether or not economic growth will increase or reduce resource-scarcity, and in what ways, is far from being a cut-and-dried question. Despite the waves of optimism and of pessimism about this subject, the issue is a constant one, with pessimism and optimism appearing to reflect short-term events. A sudden rise in energy or natural resource prices is likely to trigger off a wave of pessimism, and vice versa, and it is not only the general public that is subject to such waves but also many economists and academics. This may be because of a view that there is a genuine change in trend or because of the dangerous propensity to extrapolate short-term experience to the future. Or it may reflect, as Georgescu-Roegen (1976, p. ix) suggests, the opportunism of some economists (and other academics) as they attempt to ride on waves of public opinion. However, long-term advance of knowledge requires the following of a steadier path.

ECONOMICS, ECOLOGY, AND RESOURCES

The study of many economic problems requires attention to be paid to ecology, the discipline that examines the relationship of organisms to their surroundings or environment and to one another. There are several reasons why this is so:

1. Man is not biologically a primary producer of food but is entirely dependent on other organisms as a source of food. While man does not live

by food alone, it is essential to survival. Man lives high on the biological food chain, and the supply of food involves complex ecological relationships.

2. Not only are ecological relationships significant in satisfying the desire of man for food, but many nonfood commodities are also derived from living organisms, including timber, fibers, pharmaceuticals, chemicals, resins, leather, and so on.

3. As nonrenewable resources are depleted, man can be expected to become more dependent on other living organisms for his continued survival.

4. Not all living organisms have a favorable relationship to man and his economic activities. Pests and diseases are a part of existence and affect human welfare and economic production. Important ecological considerations may have to be taken into account in determining economic methods of controlling pests and diseases—for example, whether to use biological control methods or to engage in environmental manipulation designed to limit outbreaks of the incidence of disease.

5. The end-products of economic production and consumption are wastes that are disposed of into the environment and which can have an adverse ecological impact. These impacts need to be taken into account when planning economic activity.

6. Natural ecological relationships play an important role in providing environmental conditions suitable for the support of man; they can assist, for example, in the purification of water, the decompositin of toxic substances to harmless substances, and the maintenance of cleaner air, all of which have economic value.

7. Human welfare is not only dependent on material consumption. Many humans value forms of nature for their sheer existence or for other nonconsumptive reasons. In addition, nature is often valued for the recreational opportunities it provides. Such human desires add to the value of nature as an economic resource.

While it is true that the very possibility of man's continued existence is rooted in his ecological dependence, because he is a reliant consumer, not a primary producer, in the food web, there are, as the above listing indicates, many other reasons why resource management and resource use often require the simultaneous consideration of economics and ecology. The area of study involving the overlap of the disciplines is sometimes called ecological economics or bioeconomics (Georgescu-Roegen, 1976).

Although the focus of this book is primarily on economics, the importance of ecological relationships and biological resources for resource management and the economic consequences of destroying biological resources and their life-support systems is a major concern. Many, but not all, of the issues discussed in this book fall into the broad area of ecological economics or bioeconomics.

AN OVERVIEW OF ISSUES ADDRESSED

If one were asked to make a list of key words for this book, apart from ecological economics or bioeconomics, this would include natural resources, economic growth and development both in less developed and more developed countries, environmental economics, project evaluation and cost-benefit analysis, urban–rural migration, international migration and development, agriculture versus manufacturing, human settlements, and the development of small island nations. All the issues involve environmental interdependence in a world of change. The approach is essentially a dynamic one and is set against the backdrop of changing human experience and economic thought.

Chapter 2 provides a broad overview of changing attitudes to natural resource conservation in societies as a result of institutional and technological change. Particular attention is paid to the impact of the development of the market system and the reduced dependence on and control over the local natural resources of local communities. In general, these developments have weakened social forces favoring conservation of natural resources, including biological resources, and the recent historical experience of the Western world has most probably encouraged the notion that natural resources are virtually available in infinite supply. In general, for the last 150 years or so Western economic thought has basically reflected an optimistic view of the possibilities for continuing economic growth. Natural resource availability, and especially the availability of biological resources, have not been seen as serious constraints to continuing economic growth and advances in economic welfare. In Chapter 2 the views of economists and ecologists on the importance of biological resources for economic growth and development are contrasted, and differences in ethical attitudes toward nature are considered.

Ecologists, in contrast to economists, tend to stress the importance of sustainable ecosystems. The view that sustainability of economic growth, production, and development is desirable has become more widespread and is now accepted by a small group of economists and by several policy-makers. The concept of sustainability of economic development and production is discussed in Chapter 3. This chapter reviews broadly the parallel development of economic and recent ecological thought in relation to this subject. In particular, it pays attention to views about whether economic growth can be sustained, given limited resource availability, and whether or not less developed countries can achieve sustained economic growth and development.

In the past pessimists about the possibility of sustaining growth have mainly pointed to the depletion of nonrenewable resources, especially energy resources, as the main constraints. Chapter 4 examines the position of growth optimists and pessimists in this regard and suggests that in the foreseeable future the *availability* of energy resources is not likely to be a serious constraint on economic growth, but pollution from such sources (particularly global pollution) is likely to be a continuing serious problem, and technological advances in relation to the utilization of energy resources may not follow an optimal path. It is suggested that the most important factor for sustaining economic production and human welfare could be the conservation of our biological resources rather than the conservation of energy and other nonrenewable mineral resources.

By far the greatest number of different species of living organisms is found in Third World countries, and nowhere else. This is the case partly for biogeographic reasons: most Third World countries are located in tropical or subtropical areas, whereas more developed countries are usually in temperate areas. As one moves from the Poles toward the Equator, the number and diversity of species per unit area tends to increase. Also, the lack of economic growth in less developed countries has meant somewhat less disturbance of natural habitats, which has in turn meant the survival of a large range of species. However, economic, social, and technical changes in Third World countries are now threatening the continuing existence of many species and are leading to the destruction of their natural habitats such as tropical rainforests. These developments have consequences, economic and otherwise, not only for the less developed countries themselves, but also for the rest of the world. These consequences are discussed in Chapter 5, along with ways in which developed countries can assist the Third World in the conservation of nature and natural resources.

Man now has the ability to extinguish many species or to save them from extinction. Because of man's increased power over nature and because of the likelihood that economic change will result in the continuing loss of species, there is a need to choose which species should be preserved or, in certain circumstances, to decide whether to preserve a species in a locality or to permit unconstrained economic development, which will result in its loss. Various approaches have been suggested for determining whether or not to save a particular species from extinction. These include the guidelines set out in the World Conservation Strategy (IUCN, 1980), cost–benefit analysis, and the safe minimum standard criterion. These approaches to evaluation are assessed in Chapter 6, which also considers the possible economic importance of maintaining genetic diversity in general.

Chapter 7 involves a case study in the economics of nature conservation. It discusses the economic benefits to be obtained from conserving the yellow-eyed penguin and other wildlife species on the Otago Peninsula on the South Island of New Zealand. The yellow-eyed penguin is at least endangered locally and may be threatened globally. Economic benefits in terms of generation of tourism, regional income–employment multipliers, existence value, and benefits in relation to costs are considered. The World Conservation Strategy guidelines, cost–benefit analysis, and the safe minimum standard criterion are applied to this case.

Both economics and ecology are usually involved in the evaluation of methods to control pests, particularly for classical methods of biological control, which usually involve the import of biocontrol agents from abroad. For example, the import of insects to control weeds was used very successfully to control the prickly pear cactus in Australia. But before such a method is applied, it needs to be carefully evaluated from an economic viewpoint, especially since it can have an irreversible unfavorable economic impact. The usefulness of cost–benefit analysis for this purpose is discussed in Chapter 8, along with the shortcomings and strengths of this method, as well as of other methods used by natural scientists for evaluation of this form of pest control.

Of course, scarcity and human welfare does not depend only on the availability and use of natural resources. The quality and allocation of the human population, the human resource, and of man-made resources, such as capital, are also important; Chapters 9 and 10 give attention to these. In Chapter 9, issues such as the economics of urban–rural migration, of the optimal allocation of labor between rural and urban areas and between agriculture and manufacturing, and the optimal distribution of population between regions or settlements are discussed. All involve important questions about economic development and have consequences for economic scarcity. Lewis's agricultural labor surplus model provides a useful introduction to this chapter, even though this model is criticized and is considered to be inadequate. Specific alternatives to his model are reviewed.

Chapter 9 provides a useful backdrop to Chapter 10, which considers, among others, international migration from resource-poor small island states as a strategy for providing economic assistance to the inhabitants of such states. This migration strategy is compared with the use of foreign aid for capital accumulation and technological change in small developing island states, and also with foreign aid for income support. The problems considered are particularly relevant to small island nations in the Pacific and the Caribbean and to the developed countries that are the chief aid donors to such countries. It is argued that the natural resource-poverty and other natural disadvantages of many developing small island states mean that the direction of all or the bulk of foreign aid to capital accumulation and technological change is likely to be relatively inefficient as a means of raising the per capita income of the inhabitants of such states. This contrasts with standard or conventional trust in the effectiveness of such policies. Policies that optimists see as being effective on a global scale to reduce scarcity and overcome natural resource limits are viewed by many as also being effective in enabling small island states to develop with foreign aid. The development and economic growth problems of small island states may, to some extent, mirror in microcosm the economic difficulties that could come to be experienced globally as a result of resource depletion. However, even if this is not the case, small island states raise several important issues about economic development. The final chapter of this book provides a concluding assessment of the resource-issues and touches on important aspects of population policy.

Thus the main focus of this book is on natural resource and environmental issues arising in and from economic growth, development, and change, and on the economic importance of living or biological resources and the ethical questions involved in their conservation. Nevertheless, social as well as natural dimensions of environmental change and of choices about resource use are also given considerable attention.

2

Conserving Our Biological Resources:
Economics, Ecology, and Ethics

BACKGROUND: LACK OF CONCERN FOR CONSERVATION DUE TO THE NATURE OF WESTERN ECONOMIC DEVELOPMENT, SYSTEMS, AND VALUES

While many tribal and village people in their traditional settings are well aware of the value of conserving biological resources and have devised effective conservation methods (Johannes, 1981; Klee, 1980), the Western World on the whole has shown a noncaring and quite often destructive attitude towards nature as a product of the nature of its economic systems, its historical experience, and its Judaeo-Christian value system. Let us consider these aspects.

The economic growth of the West has largely been based upon its success with exploitative technologies, which rely heavily on the use of nonrenewable resources, especially on energy resources such as coal and oil. For more than two centuries, these nonrenewable resources have proven to be more than adequate for the economic growth of the West; furthermore, discoveries of new lands and the colonial and imperial expansion of the West made possible by its superior technologies provided it with access to a growing resource base from its viewpoint. In relation to such vast and growing power over resources (including those of other peoples), loss of any particular natural resource might justifiably have been regarded as inconsequential; more than adequate underexploited resources remained at the frontiers of new territories to compensate for any losses. Furthermore, as new technology had already overcome so many obstacles to economic growth, why should it not continue to overcome any that might arise in the future? So the historical experience of the West suggested that no particular attention need be paid to nature conservation—available resources were virtually available in infinite supply, and technological optimism was justified.

The economic systems that developed in the West in conjunction with the Industrial Revolution as well as new political systems reinforced the lack of concern for conservation of nature. Industrial production systems divorced men from nature and their dependence upon it. Manufacturing industry grew, and its efficiency required division of labor and specialization in production. Economies of scale dictated larger workforces in factories and their location in urban areas, as did the economics of tertiary industries. So the bulk of the population and the captains of industry became urbanized and alienated from nature.

Furthermore, the market system developed as a method of organizing production and the exchange of commodities. This led to divided responsibility for production as a whole and for its effects on the environment. Overall lack of knowledge arising out of the market system further diminished moral responsibility for the impact of production on the environment. The market system operates on the principle that each individual should follow his or her own self-interest, narrowly defined. The individual is not expected "to be his brother's keeper," nor to accept responsibility for social or environmental spillovers or externality from his or her individual actions. It is an impersonal system, and one of its virtues is claimed to be that it minimizes the amount of knowledge required for efficient economic decision-making.

If one buys paper, for example, it is only necessary to know the price of paper and qualities of paper for sale to make an efficient decision. It is not necessary to know anything about the primary producer of that paper, nor about the environmental efforts stemming from the production of this paper and from the harvesting of trees to supply it. Without such knowledge, no moral responsibility for environmental consequences of one's decision seems possible. And there is no economic incentive for an individual to seek such knowledge. Furthermore, even if some knowledge is available, the remoteness of production from the location of the purchaser may reduce any feeling of responsibility for environmental effects. In addition, each purchaser is liable to argue that his or her purchase is very small in relation to total production, so for all intents and purposes it is inconsequential in itself. Finally, the individual may argue that as society is competitive and motivated by self-interest as a whole, if he or she does not take economic advantage of a situation, someone else will.

With the development of the market system, mobility of labor and of people generally has increased rapidly. Individuals are no longer tied to their local communities, to their current occupations (or that of their parents), or to their current sources of earning a living in a particular location. Degradation or exhaustion of resources that support their local community or their livelihood in a particular location has become of little concern to people because they believe that they can always move to other resources as yet less degraded. But this assumption of sufficient natural resources elsewhere may prove untenable in the long run as all act on the same principle. It is difficult to escape the conclusion that increased mobility of people with the development of the market system in the West has been a major force weakening motives for and social concern about the conservation of natural resources.

However, there are further sources of diminished social responsibility present in the economic system. Various institutional changes in business enterprises have added to divided or shared responsibility and have resulted in important decision-makers and economic beneficiaries being able to escape most of the environmental consequences of their productive enterprise. The growth of the joint stock company and the operation of ownership and management of companies divides responsibility for the enterprise. Shareholders may individually feel little responsibility for the environmental consequences of the company. They may argue that they are one among many shareholders, they have little power over management, and it would be too costly to try to exert more influence, or the company will be taken over by more rapacious investors if it forgoes profit in the interest of environmental conservation.

Even management itself may find it difficult to accept environmental responsibility. It can resort to the argument that if it adopts a benign attitude to the environment, it may not be able to compete in the market with other companies that do not take this attitude. Or, if it does not maximize the return on its capital by exploiting all available environmental opportunities, it may be taken over by a financial raider (cf. Marris, 1964). Furthermore, responsibility for management in large modern corporations, particularly in multinational companies, is divided, diminishing individual responsibility for production decisions. The major decision-makers are often located a considerable distance away from a company's productive activities; they themselves do not suffer local environmental effects from their production, and, not being members of the local community, they may escape social pressures from it. Thus constraints on their behavior are reduced.

The growth of the nation states and centralized methods of governing these has also undermined local responsibility for environmental control. In many cases, this has resulted in an increase in the rate of disappearance of natural resources, because controlling government officers are out of touch with field conditions and the local community. This, for example, is reputed to have occurred in the Mount Everest area when village control of forests and trees was replaced by the control of the Forest Department, with its headquarters in Katmandu (Jefferies, 1982).

As a rule, where Western technologies, social systems of organizing production, and methods of government have come into contact with traditional communities, they have eroded local values, conservation ethics, and customs (cf. Jefferies, 1982; Tisdell, 1983b, 1986). These contacts usually provide dramatic examples of the adverse consequences on nature preservation of Western systems and values (Klee, 1980). Furthermore, traditional people have been changed in their outlook from ecosystem people to biosphere people, as defined by Raymond Dasmann and discussed by Klee (ibid., Chapter 1). They have become part to some extent of the "global technological civilization, drawing support not from the resources of any one ecosystem but from the entire biosphere" (ibid., p. 2).

However, it would be wrong to believe that all early or all non-Western civilizations have lived or live in perfect harmony with nature, conserving it and caring for it. As, for example, Blainey (1976, p. 58) points out in relation to the Australian aboriginals, "In the wiping out of certain species of giant marsupials the arrival of aboriginals and their weapons and firesticks were possibly part of the web of death. Certainly there is no justification for the assumption—widespread in the 1970s—that the aboriginals lived in complete harmony with the natural environment." In New Zealand the Maoris are reported to have extinguished the flightless moa; several species may well have been wiped out by early man in North America (ibid., p. 57).

Day (1981, p. 21) describes the Polynesian (Maori) invaders of New Zealand as an active and aggressive people, who soon formed a "moa-hunting culture." The impact of the Maoris on the population of moas "was nothing short of catastrophic"—by around 1850, the moas appear to have been wiped out by the Maoris. In Madagascar, early man is reported to have been instrumental in the disappearance of the elephant bird (*Aepyornis maximus*). While hunting played a part, egg collecting by the Malagasy people played a much bigger role in the extinction of that species (ibid., p. 29).

In Hawaii, some honeyeaters were valued by the Polynesians for their feathers and were accordingly sought after. Day (ibid., p. 102) reports that, in the case of "the spectacular Mamo *Drepanis pacifica* which had always been pursued for its black and yellow plumage, the fabric of royal Hawaiian cloaks, it was rapidly hunted into extinction after the introduction of European firearms." In this case it was the introduction of new technology from Europe that was of central importance.

The problem of a lack of concern for nature is not peculiar to the Western market system; it is evident also in state socialism, which is also a product of the Western world if it is accepted that most of its social philosophers came from this world and that Russia belongs to it. The socialist system puts great faith in the ability of men to overcome economic obstacles through effort, cooperation, and the use of capital; by centralizing major production systems and by dividing and sharing responsibility, it removes individual and local responsibility for many decisions. It therefore weakens local control and concern for the environment and may result in an uncaring attitude towards nature. In the past, state socialist leaders such as Stalin have shown themselves to be technological optimists and have exhibited arrogant attitudes to nature.

The goal of Western man in interacting directly with nature has usually been to subdue it. The Judaeo-Christian view, for instance, expressed in Genesis, is that God intends man to dominate nature. While Judaeo-Christian thought also emphasizes the unity of man with nature and God's care for all of his creation, this strand has not been dominant (cf. Daly, 1980).

Only in the last two decades has a sizeable group in the West become convinced of man's responsibility to act as steward to nature (Passmore, 1974). This group believes that man must reach a more harmonious balance with nature, either in his own self-interest, or because other sentient beings have rights to existence and consideration. As a result, (1) a search has begun in the West to specify the ethical foundations of the rights of other sentient beings; and (2) considerable effort is being made to specify the benefits to man of nature conservation and the costs to man of failing to take account of ecological considerations.

A notable relatively recent development in that respect is the *World Conservation Strategy*, drawn up by the International Union for the Conservation of Nature and Natural Resources (IUCN, 1980) in cooperation with a number of bodies of the United Nations after consultation with organizations and individuals, mostly ecologists, in more than 100 countries. It argues that it is in the economic self-interest of man to conserve biological resources and suggests that economic growth and conservation of living resources are compatible, provided proper account is taken of the ecological consequences of economic choices. It suggests that sustainable economic development is desirable but can only be achieved by conserving biological resources. This is said to require: (1) the maintenance of essential ecological processes and their support systems, for instance, in agriculture, forestry, and aquatic environments; (2) the preservation of genetic diversity; and (3) the sustainable utilization of species and ecosystems.

The World Conservation Strategy document calls attention to the deteriorating biological resource-base of the world, warns of the possible adverse economic consequences, and suggests policies to cope with the situation. It recognizes that present societies are essentially man-centered in outlook and dominated by the motive of self-interest and proceeds on this basis. The document provides an approach to economic development from the point of view of ecologists rather than of economists, challenging economists to respond (Tisdell, 1983a, 1988b).

More recently, the General Assembly of the United Nations requested the World Commission on Environment and Development to propose long-term environmental strategies for achieving sustainable development for the globe by the year 2000 and beyond. As indicated on the back of the paperback copy of the report, *Our Common Future* (WCED, 1987), it "serves notice that the time has come for a marriage of economy and ecology, so that governments and their people can take responsibility not just for environmental damage but for the policies that cause the damage." While liaison has begun between economics and ecology, there is still a considerable way to go before effective marriage becomes a reality.

ECONOMISTS AND BIOLOGICAL CONSERVATION

Western economic thought reflects the dominant values of Western society. Its welfare economics is entirely centered on the wants and desires of man. In the past economists have paid very little attention to the importance of biological resources for human welfare and the possible poverty that could follow from their disappearance or inappropriate use (cf. Scott, 1955). While classical economists such as Malthus (1798) and Ricardo (1817) put great emphasis on the importance of land (consisting of all natural resources), this was from the point of view of the operation of the law of diminishing returns to production. Ricardo recognized that the depletion of minerals could lead to increasing economic difficulties, and this point was taken up later by Jevons (1906), but no particular concern was expressed by eighteenth- and nineteenth-century economists about the disappearance of biological resources. While biological resources disappeared in the British Isles at a rapid rate and several species of animals became locally extinct as economic growth proceeded (Harting, 1880), this was not considered a major issue, presumably because it was felt that with increased trade and expansion of the British Empire, Britain had vast new biological resources to draw on.

Until the 1950s, the economic literature gave little or no attention to biological and ecological issues, and it was not until the 1970s that major interest in this area was shown by economists. Before the 1950s, there had been some interest in the economics of forestry and agricultural production, but then interest in the over-exploitation of fishery resources grew, and economic policies to deal with this problem were suggested (e.g. by Gordon, 1954). However, interest was focused on how to improve the management of biological resources so as to raise *material* welfare through changes in production.

This materialistic approach of economists in dealing with man's relationship to nature did not basically alter until the 1970s. Then critiques were produced of GDP (Gross Domestic Product) as a measure of welfare, and nonmaterialistic economic values of nature began to be specified—for instance, its value for outdoor recreation and its sheer existence value.

The recreational nature of national parks and similar natural environments was recognized, and Clawson (1959) and Clawson and Knetsch (1966) began to estimate this value by a travel cost approach. Furthermore, it was accepted that for much of the human population, natural sites and species could have *existence* value (Krutilla, 1967). Individuals who do not visit a site or view a species or intend to do so nevertheless value its continued existence and would be prepared to pay for it. Those, for example, who desire to save whales may desire to do so, whether or not they themselves ever come into contact with whales. In addition, nonusers who *might* wish to use a natural environment in the future might be prepared to pay a sum to preserve the environment and so keep their options open. This has been described as *option* value (Weisbrod, 1964). To this was added economic recognition of *bequest* value—the value that individuals place on saving species and natural environments for the enjoyment of future generations (Krutilla, 1967).

So economists came to recognize the importance of a number of nonmaterialistic values associated with nature. But they took a long time to do so, considering that the importance of the psychic dimension in the satisfaction of human wants or desires was recognized by the end of the nineteenth century and increasingly came to be accepted within the economics profession. By the end of the 1930s, the view of Robbins (1937) was already widely accepted that economics is the science concerned with the social administration or management of scarce resources in order to satisfy human desires for commodities to the maximum extent possible. These desires might be for necessities or for nonnecessities, for physical or nonphysical objects or characteristics. However, it is a sad reflection that economists were much quicker to take account of the economic value of tobacco on this basis than that of nature conservation.

Increasing attention is being given by economists to the rationale for preserving species and irreplaceable natural environments. Arrow and Fisher (1974) point out that even if one only wishes to maximize benefit on average, there is a case for conserving natural environments to keep options open—that is, to retain flexibility. The Resources for the Future (RFF) group in the United States incorporated such considerations in a cost–benefit analysis of conservation versus development of natural environments. The RFF group aims to undertake cost–benefit analyses and to quantify in money terms all anticipated benefits and costs (to humans) of the preservation of particular species, in relation to decisions about whether to conserve a species or which species to preserve. However, the great stumbling block is to estimate future benefits with a reasonable degree of accuracy. Many biological resources that appeared in the past to have no possible future value have subsequently grown to be very valuable. We cannot always know with precision the future value of biota, and we risk through ignorance eliminating a biological resource that might prove valuable in the future, for example, in the fight against cancer or another major disease. We are involved in decision-making under uncertainty.

The existence of such uncertainty has led some economists to recommend that we should err more in favor of conservation compared to economic development than might be suggested by the Resources for the Future group. The cost–benefit analysis used by this alternative school of thought, of which Bishop (1978, 1979) is a leading advocate, has its intellectual roots in the work of Ciriacy-

Wantrup (1968), to whom major credit must go for stimulating interest in ecological economics. Basically, they argue that given uncertainty about the value of species and given that the possible value of preserving a species could exceed the costs of its conservation, the species should be preserved at a sufficient level to guarantee its continued existence. This has become known as the safe minimum standard (SMS) approach and implies a safety-first or extremely cautious attitude towards risk-taking. For those familiar with game theory, it is a minimax loss approach. Economic debate about these issues is continuing.

As suggested by Randall (1986) who presents a compromise approach the merits and drawbacks of which cannot be debated here, neither the RFF cost–benefit approach nor the SMS approach is an entirely satisfactory basis for making decisions on the preservation of species. As in our society attitudes to risk vary and differences of opinions exist about possible consequences of meddling with nature, it is difficult or impossible to achieve unanimity in decision-making involving the environment. There are fundamental differences between people in the degree of risks they believe to be appropriate to take with our environment, and this conflict is not necessarily amenable to resolution by rational argument.

Despite the expanding consideration of conservation issues by economists, the basic stand of virtually all economists is still as it was expressed by A. D. Scott in 1955:

The ultimate end of economic policy is human welfare. It follows that society must allocate and economize upon scarce resources in order to maximize the satisfaction of its given ends. "Conservation" is not accepted here as an end in itself. [Scott, 1955, p. 3]

Even when economists have argued in favor of limiting economic growth and population growth, they have done so on the basis of its benefits to mankind. Hermann Daly (1980), for instance, argues for a steady state economy (SSE) in which there is zero population growth and individuals restrain their consumption to a minimum acceptable level. He favors this strategy not because of its favorable impact on the conservation of nature but because, in his view, it will enable the human species to survive for the longest time possible. He regards the survival of the human species as the primary goal.

ECOLOGISTS AND BIOLOGICAL CONSERVATION

The ethical views of ecologists on the conservation of nature are much more varied than those of economists, and not all ecologists accept the view that the end of conservation is the satisfaction of human desires as measured by economists. As the power of man to destroy nature has become obvious and with the growing awareness of the disappearance of species and natural environments, many members of the public are looking towards ecologists to provide policy and ethical guidance lacking in their Judaeo-Christian inheritance. This has been pointed out by Worster (1975) who, after reviewing the history of ecological thought, concludes that we now live in the Age of Ecology. While this may not yet be so, ecologists and conservationists are clearly exerting a greater impact on policy than in the past.

It is not possible to review the ethical underpinnings and relevant policy conclusions of all ecological studies here. Only a few points can be noted.

First, some ecologists are man-centered in their ethics, whereas others are not. The World Conservation Strategy (IUCN, 1980) already mentioned provides an example of a man-centered approach. Basically, it argues that a degree of conservation greater than that now practised is necessary if mankind is to satisfy his desires to the maximum extent possible in a sustainable way. The approach of the Ehrlichs (Ehrlich, 1970; Ehrlich, Ehrlich, & Holdren, 1976) also appears to be man-centered; it predicts ecological, economic, and environmental doom for mankind unless population growth and economic growth are restrained. This approach is therefore similar to Daly's mentioned earlier. Other less well-known ecologists warn of dangers of collapse in agricultural production if species diversity is not maintained and point to examples of civilizations such as the Mayan, which may have collapsed due to the narrow genetic base of their crop varieties (Plucknett, Smith, Williams, & Anishetty, 1986, pp. 12–14).

Another group of ecologists and conservationists believes that nature has a right to exist independently of the wishes of man. Aldo Leopold (1933, 1966), for instance, sees man as a holistic part of an organic community. Man has no special right to exterminate parts of it. Even predatory species are a part of the web of life and should not be exterminated. In expounding his "land ethic," Leopold was expressing opposition to the narrow economic attitude toward nature management that had come to dominate ecology.

Still another group of ecologists sees ultimate value in preserving various representative biomes, ecosystems, or natural environments since either they themselves as ecologists value natural diversity or feel under some social obligation to preserve it. Rudge (1986), for example, in a presidential address to the New Zealand Ecological Society, claimed in relation to New Zealand that:

In terms of land management, the ultimate measure for ecologists is the healthy functioning of those parts of the Gondwanaland heritage which are in trust to New Zealand. . . . The public perception of nature conservation is not sufficient of itself without the more fundamental scientific values embodied in the Gondwanaland concept. [ibid., p. 1]

Rudge points out that this involves a value judgement largely by people with scientific training. His case is that "Gondwanaland is a unique evolutionary treasure entrusted to New Zealand to preserve as biological history for today's world and future generations" (Rudge, 1986, p. 6). But as a later comment by Scott (1955) indicates, this attitude cuts little ice with traditional economists.

Other aspects of ecological ideas are also worth considering. Ecologists tend to favor self-sustaining ecological systems and prefer equilibrium to disequilibrium. Some claim that the elimination of just one species might throw the whole ecological balance into disequilibrium. But, as Mentis (1984) has pointed out, disequilibrium is a natural or normal ecological state, and it helps to explain the process of evolution. Why is sustainability and equilibrium so desirable?

There is conflict between conservationists and ecologists who feel that man must manage wildlife to ensure its survival, given modified environmental conditions and those who wish to return to natural processes of wildlife management. For instance, given restriction in animal movement due to the size of the Kruger National Park—which, nevertheless, is as large as Belgium—elephants and other species have to be culled to prevent overpopulation, habitat alteration, and possible (local) extinction of some species. In order to return to "natural" processes of evolution and species interaction, we would need to return a very large fraction of the Earth to wilderness. But why are natural processes best—if they are indeed so? Since a return of a major portion of the globe to wilderness at possibly a considerable cost to man would be required to ensure the ascendency of natural processes, convincing arguments are needed in favor of this.

CONCLUDING COMMENTS

Economists have generally not been sympathetic to those ecologists who do not subscribe to their value systems. Scott (1955, p. 12) commenting on the view that natural resources are a gift to mankind by nature and held in trust, says:

This sentiment has very little direct economic significance. . . . Since the conservation of natural resources takes on in these circumstances the status of a desired objective of and for itself, no economic argument can stand against it . . . The same comment might be made about those idealists who feel with Burke that mankind should leave the earth as it was.

But these sentiments do become relevant to mainstream economists if people are willing to pay to give substance to them. Economists doing cost–benefit analyses generally use the willingness (and ability) of individuals to pay as a measure of value. While this takes account of the strength of desires of individuals for different objects, it does so only within the confines of the existing distribution of income and is subject to other limitations. Because the wealthy have a greater ability to pay, it results in their having a greater potential influence on policy choices. Except for the wealth factor, no social group, such as the scientists mentioned by Rudge (1986), have a special influence on policy. If they are willing to pay, the misinformed, as well as the informed, are given equal weight. One would therefore expect economists as individuals to be uneasy about using this criterion as an arbiter of ultimate value, and indeed significant economic thinkers such as Pigou (1932) have held this position. Economic values can only be a partial guide to social decision-making.

Neither economists nor ecologists have been able to supply us with a wholly convincing set of values and ethics, and it is doubtful whether they will be able to do so. We are engaged, it seems, in a never-ending search for ultimate ends and values, and it may be—as historicism suggests—that many of our beliefs are products of their times (Worster, 1985, p. 345). The fact that I should address this subject as an economist is not only a reflection of my own personal values in favor of conservation, but a reflection of changing attitudes in Western society toward nature conservation and the environment and the developing interest of a growing band of economists in these issues.

Finally, let me state in conclusion by way of an example that the biological resources and natural environments of the south of the South Island of New Zealand are clearly of considerable economic value. This is obvious for its fisheries and its national parks and natural landscapes, but the economic potential of its wildlife resources should not be underrated, whether one has in mind the existence value of the takahe or the economic value of wildlife for tourism. In this respect wildlife in the Otago Peninsula has great potential. The value to Dunedin of the Royal Albatross colony at Taiaroa Head as a tourist attraction is now widely recognized. But there is more scope for economic gains to be made from tourism by conserving and setting aside protected areas for additional species on the Otago Peninsula, such as the yellow-eyed penguin. Dunedin is fortunate to have such a valuable range of biological wildlife resources in close proximity, which it can, if it wishes, choose to conserve and manage for its economic gain, and thereby also contribute to the preservation of species (see the case study in Chapter 7).

3

Sustainable Economic Growth, Production, and Development: Concepts and Changing Views

The question of whether economic growth can be sustained in perpetuity and which factors, if any, limit economic growth has been debated for more than three centuries. Following the publication of Malthus' essay on population in 1798 and the publication of Ricardo's *Principles of Political Economy and Taxation* in 1817, the proposition that economic growth and development are likely to be limited by population growth and especially by constraints imposed by the limited productivity of land or natural resources was of major concern. But toward the end of the last century this concern began to wane, with the rise of the neoclassical school of economics and the sustained economic growth of center countries like Great Britain. Natural resources were no longer viewed as serious impediments to sustaining economic growth. Capital accumulation and to a lesser extent technological progress were seen as sufficient to overcome any barriers that might be posed by natural resources. While emphasis changed, this view basically prevailed without any serious challenge until the 1970s, when it was increasingly challenged by the so-called neo-Malthusians. This group began to emphasize once more the importance of natural resources as setting limits to economic growth. Like the original "Malthusians," they see the limited productivity of land as a constraint on economic growth, but they place much greater stress on the finiteness of nonrenewable resources such as minerals and especially energy resources as limiting economic growth. However, they also bring new issues into the debate:

1. the possibility that environmental pollution arising directly as a by-product of economic production might choke off production and threaten human populations and their life-support systems on a global scale;
2. the disappearance of living resources, such as forests, and the growing extinction of species and loss of biological diversity as a result of economic growth may mean that economic growth and production cannot be sustained and global environmental hazards might result.

While neo-Malthusians differ somewhat in their views, most agree that *sustainable* economic development is desirable and that if economic growth is to take place, it should also be sustainable. This is the policy position taken in the *World Conservation Strategy* document (IUCN, 1980) and more recently in *Our Common Future* (World Commission on Environment and Development, 1987), a report called for by the General Assembly of the United Nations. It is therefore worthwhile considering the possible meanings of the concept of sustainability as applied to economic growth, production, and development, since most advocates of sustainability fail to do this. By not doing so, they risk a vague and non-operational approach to policy.

The concept of sustainability as applied recently to economic growth, production, and development having been examined, a review of changes in economic thought about the sustainability of economic growth and development is made, beginning with the early Malthusian/anti-Malthusian debate. The discussion then covers neoclassical economic theories, post-Keynesian and neo-Marxist views, equilibrium-trap theories, and, finally, the concerns of neo-Malthusians. Only a thumbnail sketch can be provided of changing economic thought, but the focus will be on changing attitudes to natural resources as constraints on economic growth.

SUSTAINABILITY AS A CONCEPT

From the 1970s onward, the desirability of sustainable development has been increasingly stressed as a goal. Barbier (1987) points out that the 1972 United Nations Conference on the Human

Environment held in Stockholm is usually credited with populariz-
ing the concept of sustainable development and states that "it may
be extremely difficult, if not impossible, to define sustainable
development in any analytically rigorous way" (ibid., p. 131). *The
World Conservation Strategy* (IUCN, 1980) places additional
emphasis on the concept. It suggests that "the maintenance of
essential ecological processes and life-support systems, the preservation of genetic diversity, and the sustainable utilization of species
and ecosystems" are needed to achieve "sustainable development
through the conservation of living resources." Conway (1985) suggests that sustainability of agricultural yields of production is an
important characteristic to be taken into account when deciding
whether to introduce new agricultural techniques or systems, and
debate continues about whether unlimited economic growth can be
sustained. The concept of sustainability permits many interpretations. If useful guidelines and debates about policy are to emerge
from it, relevant interpretations need to be specified more precisely
than in the past. We need to specify: (1) what characteristics or
variables should be sustainable; (2) whether they should be sustainable in perpetuity or for a shorter period of time; and (3) the
extent to which it is desirable for a system or variables to be able to
withstand shocks and recover to a level that can be sustained—that
is, the extent to which resilience is required.

It is much easier to specify these characteristics in relation to
production and economic growth than for development, because
development is multidimensional. However, some progress in
defining sustainability may be made by relating it to concepts of
equilibrium.

Economists are aware from model building that equilibrium
values in economic systems are sustainable in the absence of disturbances. But this in itself is not very significant. We must also
consider the stability or otherwise of an equilibrium (cf. Tisdell,
1972). If some shock or disturbance occurs to the system, will it
return to the state of equilibrium? If so, how quickly will it return?
Furthermore, is the equilibrium stable in the case of disturbances of
a small magnitude but unstable in the face of major disturbances?
What I am suggesting here is that the concept of sustainability,
which is basically a product of ecological thought in the present
growth and development debate, can be sharpened by relating it to
concepts of equilibrium and stability of equilibrium as used in

economic models. Presumably a highly sustainable level of production or rate of economic growth constitutes a state of equilibrium and is strongly stable, with dynamic mechanisms that quickly return it to equilibrium once it is disturbed (cf. Tisdell, 1988).

But of course equilibrium and sustainability are not in themselves necessarily ideal. While in some economic models equilibria have been associated with an economic ideal (e.g. the Paretian ideal corresponding to conditions of equilibrium in perfectly competitive markets) in other economic models this is not so, as, for instance, the unemployment equilibrium of Keynesian models and the low per capita income equilibrium trap in some underdeveloped countries as expounded in Leibenstein's theory of underdevelopment (Leibenstein, 1957). Basically, most economists do not regard equilibrium and sustainability as being valuable characteristics in themselves. This is underlined by the approach of most economists to the optimal use of natural resources. Optimality is usually claimed to require maximization of the discounted present value of the resource—an approach pioneered by Irving Fisher (1930). Cost–benefit analyses based on this principle imply in some circumstances that it is optimal to exhaust or use up a resource completely within a relatively short period of time so that the resource eventually sustains no production or little production. As Clark (1976) has pointed out, if the rate of growth in value of production from a living resource is less than the rate of interest, it may be optimal from an economic point of view to extinguish this resource completely, so that it can no longer sustain any production. On this basis, it may be optimal from an economic viewpoint to extinguish some living species, such as slow-growing types of trees or fish species. Even though a few economists (Ciriacy-Wantrup, 1968; Bishop, 1978) have cautioned against such a narrow approach because uncertainties and externalities are ignored, the mainstream economic viewpoint remains that sustainability of natural resource use, even renewable resource use, is not a worthwhile goal in itself and, indeed, may reduce human welfare rather than add to it.

While the concept of sustainable economic growth and sustainable levels of production can, with some effort, be refined by drawing on concepts of equilibrium and stability, it is more difficult to do this for the concept of sustainable development, unless one restricts attention to *economic* development and defines this narrowly in terms of rising levels of real per capita income and, say, subject to those below an absolute poverty line not increasing in number (cf. Meier, 1976, p. 6). But development involves the *total* development of society, not just its economic development. Barbier (1987, p. 103) contends that sustainable economic development "is indistinguishable from the total development of society and cannot effectively be analysed separately, as 'sustainability' depends upon the interaction of economic changes with social, cultural and ecological transformations." He argues that total development depends upon interaction between three systems:

1. the biological (and other natural resource) system;
2. the economic system; and
3. the social system.

Human-ascribed goals apply in relation to each of these systems and must be taken into account simultaneously in determining a path or paths of sustainable development. Barbier suggests that goals in relation to each of these three systems might be:

1. for the *biological system*, maintenance of genetic diversity, resilience, and biological productivity;
2. for the *economic system*, the satisfaction of basic needs (reducing poverty), equity-enhancement, increasingly useful goods and services;
3. for the *social system*, ensuring cultural diversity, institutional sustainability, social justice, and participation.

He claims that all the systems and goals need to be considered simultaneously. Furthermore, he claims that conventional economists have been very narrow in their approach, as they have only taken account of economic systems. Marxist economists have had a somewhat wider perspective because they have tried to take account of both economic and social systems. Nevertheless, in his view, both groups of economists have failed to take account of biological systems in considering development issues.

As can be seen from the historical sketch below, Barbier's assertion about neglect of biological systems when applied in this century to economic thought by economists does have foundation. On the other hand, it should be pointed out that Barbier (1987) has not produced an operational concept of sustainable development. In particular, the issue of how trade-offs between goals are to be handled and the nature of interaction between the three systems need more attention. Yet it is clear that an economic system that abuses biological resources and creates or depends on a social system that is itself unsustainable will in turn become unsustainable. The interdependence of systems cannot be ignored if we are to avoid the possibility of serious mistakes about optimal development policy.

THE RICARDIAN/MALTHUS GROWTH MODEL AND MARX'S REACTION TO IT

While Barbier (1987) claims that conventional economists have neglected biological factors and constraints, this claim is not valid for the theories of the classical economists, T. R. Malthus (1798) and David Ricardo (1817). Both saw supply-side factors due to the "niggardliness of nature" as the main constraint on unlimited economic growth. Their view of constraints imposed by biological resources and other natural resources may not now be regarded as highly sophisticated, but the essential biological bases of their theories are clear.

As is well known, Malthus proposed that human population tends to increase in proportion to the means of subsistence, and that in practice population tends to increase in a geometric progression and production in an arithmetic progression. In the long run, population increases to a level that just ensures a subsistence level of income for the surviving population. This view considerably influenced the development of ecological thought (Worster, 1985) and was expanded into a complete theory by David Ricardo. This model, as Kindleberger (1965, p. 41) stresses, emphasized the limits to growth imposed by land.

Although land included all natural resources (all gifts of God or nature), Ricardo clearly believed agricultural land to be of prime importance and concentrated on illustrating his theory by reference to it. In his view, as production expands, diminishing returns to resource-use can be expected, both from a more intensive use of existing agricultural land and from the extension of agricultural production to inferior land. Given diminishing returns to agricultural production and the Malthusian theory of population and the absence of technological progress, an economy will come into long-term equilibrium when the level of population and aggregate production is such that per-capita income equals the subsistence level of income. While this stationary state or long-term equilibrium could be staved off by technological progress, Ricardo believed that technological progress would give only temporary respite.

It should be noted that Ricardo's limit to growth depends upon a static law of diminishing productivity. In fact, Ricardo regards the natural properties of agricultural land as indestructible and the stationary state as *sustainable* in perpetuity. Thus limits to growth do not arise out of natural resource depletion, from a reduction in the living resource base, or from the use of nonrenewable resources such as minerals, even though Ricardo was aware that the use of minerals could reduce the available stock and might pose a constraint to sustained growth or maintenance of a steady-state.

Marx and Engels strongly disagree with the pessimistic view expressed by Malthus and Ricardo about the sustainability of economic growth. They believed that as a result of scientific and technological progress production would increase at least as fast as population and possibly faster (Tisdell, 1981), and unlimited economic growth was to be expected. All constraints that might be imposed by nature and by population increase could be overcome by scientific progress according to this optimistic viewpoint. In Marx's view the poverty of the masses had its origin in the exploitative character of the capitalist system rather than in the constraints imposed by the niggardliness of nature and by population growth.

NEOCLASSICAL AND ASSOCIATED GROWTH MODELS, POST-KEYNESIAN MODELS

By the turn of the last century, the Ricardian theory of economic growth no longer played a central role in economic thought. As Kindleberger (1965, p. 45) points out, part of the reason was that "economic growth proceeded so effectively in Western Europe and North America, despite the bogey of Ricardian diminishing returns." Increasingly, land was not seen as a limiting factor to growth. Growth-reducing factors, such as economies of scale (both external and internal, especially in manufacturing), entrepreneurship, and later improvements in the quality of the factors of production, labor, and capital, and technological change, came to be stressed. Growth models came *typically* to include capital and labor as major considerations and to exclude land as a constraint on economic growth. Neoclassical economic growth models reached a high level of mathematical development during the late 1950s and early 1960s, following the development of significant post-Keynesian economic growth models in the 1940s.

Following the Great Depression of the 1930s, the attention of economists in more developed capitalist countries turned to the problem of how to maintain full employment. Insufficiency of aggregate demand was seen as a possibly persistent phenomenon, which could prevent capitalist economies from achieving full employment and reaching their potential levels of output and economic growth. Demand-side rather than supply-side factors were now considered to be the main constraint on achieving full employment and maximizing economic growth. Harrod (1939, 1948) developed a model in which capital and labor, the only inputs, are required in constant proportions for production and in which constant returns to scale prevail (cf. Jones, 1975, see 3.2). This model, within the ambit of its assumptions, demonstrates that a capitalist economy would be unlikely to generate a steady or sustainable rate of growth ensuring full employment. Hicks (1949) further "refined" this model to demonstrate how it can or is likely to generate cycles of economic activity. Given these cycles, maximum economic growth and production are achieved only for a very short time and intermittently. Generally production is below its potential because of insufficiency of aggregate demand. In that model, Hicks also implicitly displays an optimistic view of economic growth potential. The lines of basic economic growth potential in his model "slope" upwards as a function of time. The general implication of these models is that demand, at least in developed countries, is the chief constraint on economic growth, and production constraints imposed by the niggardliness of nature are not a problem. The assumption used in these models is that constant returns to scale in production prevail in relation to the use of labor and capital. It implies that land or natural resources do not restrict production. If anything, the focus is on capital as a constraint on growth. If the rate of capital accumulation can be made to proceed at the same rate as the growth of the labor force (which Harrod thought to be unlikely), production in the economy (given these models) will grow at a constant proportional rate, and a so-called "Golden Age" will be sustainable if full employment is achieved.

Neoclassical economists reacted to the Harrod-Domar model and variants of this post-Keynesian model by arguing that its assumption that labor and capital cannot be substituted in production is unrealistic. Solow (1956) relaxed this assumption while retaining the other assumptions of the Harrod-Domar model, thus instituting a "renaissance" for the neoclassical approach and reaching an optimistic conclusion about economic growth. He argued that once substitutability is allowed for, there are mechanisms in the economy to ensure that the rate of economic growth converges to the same rate as the rate of increase in the labor force. The problem of sustaining economic growth as expounded by the post-Keynesians disappears.

But Solow (ibid.) takes no account of natural resource constraints. Only capital and labor count in terms of production and via the Cobb–Douglas production function ensure constant returns to scale. Economic growth in aggregate production can be sustained in perpetuity at a rate equal to the rate of population increase, assuming that the labor force is a constant proportion of the population. In this model an increased propensity to save can raise aggregate production in relation to a given population and raise income per head, but the long-run or equilibrium rate of growth remains unchanged at the rate of growth of the labor force (cf. Jones, 1975, p. 84). Income per head can be raised by more capital accumulation per capita. Furthermore, there is no population problem in the long run. Population can grow in perpetuity and income per capita can be sustained in perpetuity according to this model. Population and natural resource constraints of the Ricardian model entirely disappear at this stage of economic thought. But the matter did not rest there.

Solow (1956) had not taken technological progress explicitly into account. Attention among neoclassical growth theorists soon turned to this matter, and Solow (1957) emphasized that technological progress or a "residual" factor was the major contributor to economic growth in the United States. Considerable discussion and development of ideas about the relative contribution of quantitative factors and qualitative factors to economic growth ensued (see, for example, Jones, 1975, Chapters 7 and 8). If anything, by attention to technological progress and qualitative factors the view that economic growth, including population growth, could proceed in perpetuity and that natural resources would provide no real constraint to this process was strengthened.

LOW-LEVEL EQUILIBRIUM TRAP, NEO-MARXIANS, AND ECONOMIC GROWTH IN LESS DEVELOPED COUNTRIES

Mainstream economic thought commencing with the post-Keynesian growth theorists and continuing with subsequent neoclassical growth theorists tends to take a dichotomous view of economic growth in more developed countries (MDCs) as compared to that in less developed countries (LDCs). Problems and models of economic growth applicable to MDCs are frequently considered not to be applicable to LDCs and vice versa, and some theorists believe that growth theory as developed for MDCs has little relevance to the economics of underdevelopment (Jones, 1975, pp. 4–5).

Be this as it may, some economic theorists, for instance Rostow (1960), suggested that many LDCs are trapped in a stationary state with characteristics typical of those in the Ricardian model. But by a "Big-Push" or a "critical minimum effort" such as a large injection of foreign aid it might be possible for an LDC to escape from its low-level equilibrium-trap and to achieve sustained economic growth. Once take-off into (sustained) economic growth occurs in a country, this growth is envisaged as continuing in perpetuity, and the country eventually joins the MDC league. There are no limits to economic growth, but the basic problem in LDCs is to get the process of sustained economic growth started.

Leibenstein (1957) pointed out that the matter of escaping from a low-equilibrium trap was not as straightforward as imagined by some theorists. A very large increase in per capita income might be needed to escape the trap (see ibid., p. 98, Figure 8.1a). Again, global stability of low-level per-capita income equilibrium could not be ruled out, nor could its global upward instability (ibid., Figures

8.1b and 8.1c). In the latter case, just a small increase in per-capita income so as to bring it above the low-level equilibrium level would be sufficient to result in sustained economic growth. An upshot of the discussion was that LDCs should concentrate on creating conditions that will raise induced income growth and/or lower induced income declines as a function of per-capita income, thereby reducing the minimum critical effort needed to escape from the low-equilibrium trap. Alternatively, or also, they should seek aid from developed countries that might assist such an escape.

However, a number of neo-Marxians (e.g., Frank, 1978) and some non-Marxians objected that aid from and economic contact with MDCs, far from making it easier for LDCs to escape from their low-level equilibrium-trap, would make it more difficult for them to do so. Such contact could reduce induced income growth as a function of per capita income and raise induced income declines as a function of per capita income. Such shifts or tilts in these relationships (the X_c and Z_c functions, as described by Leibenstein, 1957) can either be expected to increase the level of minimum critical effort needed to escape from the low-level equilibrium trap or even to convert a low-level equilibrium that is inherently unstable upwards into one that is globally stable, so ruling out the possibility of sustained economic growth for the LDC. As, for the example suggested by Maitra (1986, 1988a), contact of an LDC with MDCs may weaken its propensity to develop indigenous technology, thereby weakening one force for induced income growth. It is not the purpose here to debate the merits of the various positions but merely to note that constraints from natural resources and land do not feature as a significant constraint to development within these models. At least once sustained growth begins, land is not regarded as a limiting factor.

Most economists were convinced by the 1970s (and most may still be) that natural resources and biological resources do not constitute significant constraints to sustained economic growth. If natural resources are important, most economists thought this would be so only in the early stages of growth, but as economic growth proceeds the importance of the supply of natural resources declines and in more developed countries they are a negligible constraint (cf. Kindleberger, 1965, p. 62). Even in 1965, Kindleberger describes such resources or land as "the indestructible gift of nature" (ibid., p. 62), which shows a lack of awareness at least of land depletion—for example, soil erosion, disappearance of forests and of species, and the possible consequences of this for sustaining economic growth. The emergence of neo-Malthusian concerns about limits to economic growth and to development, which gathered momentum in the 1970s, came as a surprise and a challenge to virtually the whole economic profession. Neither conventional economists nor Marxists believed that there were biological or natural resource constraints that might limit continuing economic growth.

NEO-MALTHUSIANS AND SUSTAINABLE ECONOMIC GROWTH AND DEVELOPMENT

Towards the end of the 1960s, two new issues began to be raised by a small group of economists. They began (1) to question whether continuing economic growth in MDCs is desirable (Mishan, 1967), and (2) to suggest that there were limits to economic growth arising out of possible *global* pollution from production and from depletion of nonrenewable natural resources, especially energy resources (Boulding, 1966; Georgescu-Roegen, 1971). A number of non-economists also developed this theme, combining it with the Ricardian principle of diminishing marginal returns and stressing the population problem (Ehrlich, 1970; Ehrlich et al., 1976; Forrester, 1971). The economists Daly and Georgescu-Roegen also expressed their concern. Daly (1980) proposed that in order to ensure the longest possible period of survival of the human race, use of minerals should be restricted, a zero rate of population should be aimed for, and consumption per capita should be held to a minimum acceptable level rather than maximized. (For a discussion of this approach, see Tisdell, 1988b). Georgescu-Roegen (1971, especially Section 3, Chapter 10) goes further and suggests that actual human populations may need to be reduced rather than stabilized to ensure the maximum period of existence of the human species. He bases his view on the entropy law of physics. Economic growth relies on high entropy (concentrated) energy, which it uses and disperses. Eventually the stock of such resources will be completely dispersed and no longer available for production. In Georgescu-Roegen's view, unlimited economic growth is in principle impossible, and there is no possibility of human invention (technological progess) making it so because of the operation of the basic principle of entropy.

The possibility of sustaining unlimited economic growth has also started to be questioned from an ecological viewpoint. Ecological growth can lead to reduced biological diversity, and this may limit its sustainability. Much of economic production relies on biological or living resources. Not only are many of these resources being reduced in quantity or bio-mass, but species and varieties are disappearing at a rapid rate primarily due to economic growth, the activities of man, and increased levels of human population. The loss of genetic diversity could make it increasingly difficult to sustain production from domesticated plants and animals. In the past, wild relatives of domesticated species have been used through cross-breeding and other methods to circumvent diseases and other threats to domesticated species. If this "wild" gene bank should disappear as a result of economic growth, economic growth itself could eventually become unsustainable.

This is one of the messages of the *World Conservation Strategy* (IUCN, 1980) which also highlights other ecological or biological factors that need to be taken into account in planning for sustainable development, even if only a relatively short planning horizon is considered. However, as suggested by Barbier (1987) and as discussed in this book, sustainable development is likely to require simultaneous account to be taken of at least three systems— namely, the biological system, the economic system, and the social system.

CONCLUDING COMMENTS

After approximately a century of optimism by economists about the possibility of unlimited economic growth unhindered by natural resource or environmental constraints, some economists and ecologists began questioning this possibility by the 1970s and continue to do so. While this group has been described as neo-Malthusians, they have developed theories and perceptions that go beyond those of Malthus and Ricardo with their emphasis on the *depletion* of natural resources, including biological resources, and on the possible limits to growth imposed by aggregate production, which causes (global) pollution and environmental deterioration.

Georgescu-Roegen has argued on the basis of fundamental physical laws that unlimited economic growth is an impossibility, and very high levels of production dependent on stock energy resources cannot be maintained *in perpetuity*.

Given the possibility that economic growth and development may be unsustainable, a search has begun to find policies that will help to promote sustainability. The *World Conservation Strategy* (IUCN, 1980) sets out some recent proposals in this regard and argues in favor of sustainable development, which, among other things, requires conservation of biological resources to be taken into consideration. The importance of this approach is also highlighted in *Our Common Future* (World Commission on Environment and Development, 1987) and in recent contributions such as Redclift (1987) and Clark and Munn (1986). However, as Barbier (1987) points out, sustainable development involves several systems or dimensions, and, as I have mentioned here and elsewhere (Tisdell, 1988b), the concept of sustainability is not well defined. It may also be that no development can be sustained forever and that sustainability in itself is not necessarily a virtue. Nevertheless, it is hard to escape the conclusion that the "neo-Malthusians" are dealing with important issues. At least they may discover policies that otherwise might not be found and which will enable us to sustain desired developments for longer than would otherwise be the case. They provide a valuable antidote to the arrogant attitudes of some economists evident for at least a century that economic growth and development can be sustained without regard for nature and without consideration of the interrelationships of economics with social and other systems.

4

Conservation in Less Developed Countries: A Matter for Concern Given Economic Pressures and Change

Although there is considerable concern about the disappearance of species and living resources in the world generally, particular concern is being expressed (especially in developed countries) about the rapid disappearance of such resources in LDCs. While the *World Conservation Strategy* (IUCN, 1980) suggests policies for conserving living resources for the world as a whole, it gives particular attention to problems and measures that can be adopted in LDCs to promote resource conservation. This raises the question, first, of why there is so much concern about conservation in LDCs; second, what the particular development and economic changes in LDCs are that are subjecting their living resources to so much pressure; and, third, why developed countries are concerned about conservation in LDCs and what assistance or aid developed countries should provide to support conservation in LDCs. Let us address each of these matters in turn.

REASONS FOR CONCERN ABOUT CONSERVATION IN LDCs

There are a number of reasons why special concern is being shown about conservation in LDCs. These include:

1. LDCs contain a considerably greater number of species than developed countries. This is because LDCs tend to be in tropical areas, whereas most developed countries tend to be in more temperate regions. The number of species per unit area rises as one moves from the poles to the equator. Biogeographically, a much larger number of species is potentially at risk in developing countries. Also, in the past the relative lack of economic growth in these countries has favored conservation of natural environments, and, in turn, this has been favorable for the preservation of the species.

2. The rate of disappearance of species and living resources seems now to be more rapid in developing countries than in developed ones, due in part to the more rapid population growth in LDCs.

3. LDCs are much more dependent on living resources for their economic well-being than developed countries, as most of their population tends to be employed in agriculture or primary production.

4. Various socioeconomic, institutional, and ethical changes in LDCs may have seriously undermined traditional social forces supporting conservation in these countries (some of these are considered later).

5. The developed world has come to realize that its access to additional stocks of living resources is now seriously limited. During the period of territorial economic expansion of the West (the "Age of Discovery" and subsequently) the availability of living resources must have appeared to be virtually limitless, and the disappearance of a particular species of little concern. The notion that the Earth is a global village or the spaceship concept as popularized by Boulding (1966) is now more widely accepted.

6. The developed world perceives that it has an interest in the conservation of living resources in developing countries as a sustainable source of supplies, as a genetic reserve, to counteract the greenhouse effect, and to provide species and environments that have existence, curiosity, and tourism value. To a large extent the West is motivated by self-interest in advocating conservation in LDCs, even though there may be circumstances where it is also in the interest of the LDC to conserve resources.

The natural resources of LDCs may be more vital for their development now than were those of developed countries in and following the phase of their take-off into economic growth. LDCs embarking on economic growth or development today may face greater resource constraints than did the developed countries prior to their development. For one thing, LDCs are not currently able to draw to as great an extent on unexploited or virgin resources, especially beyond their own territories. Consequently, they must rely more heavily on their own natural resources to commence and maintain economic growth and development or compensate in other ways, and this may make the process more difficult for them. Thus they have an extra handicap in their late start.

In recent centuries it seems that developed countries have been responsible for the disappearance of species and natural environments on the largest scale. In Britain many species of wild animals disappeared within historic times (Harting, 1880), and natural environments such as oak forests were much reduced due to economic growth. British settlement abroad and exploitation of world resources added to this process on a global scale. This pattern was repeated in and by other European nations.

The question might be asked whether such disappearance of living resources is an inevitable consequence of economic growth. If it is, are individuals in developed countries justified in calling for greater conservation in LDCs? Such calls are being made at present on the basis that economic development that neglects the conservation of living resources and their support system is likely to be unsustainable (IUCN, 1980).

Raymond Dasmann (Klee, 1980) has referred to people in traditional societies as "ecosystem people" and those in developed countries as "biosphere people"—the former dependent on local ecosystems and the latter relying on the world's resources as a whole. It is argued (ibid.) that ecosystem people are highly motivated to sustain ecosystems, whereas biosphere people are not. To what extent is it feasible and desirable for communities in LDCs to change from being ecosystem people (in favor of conservation) to being biosphere people? Will the possible economic gains from international trade compensate for reduced ecological and possibly reduced economic sustainability? These are difficult questions to answer, but our discussion will throw light on the matter.

It is sometimes supposed that *all* traditional societies are imbued with a strong conservation ethic and engage in desirable conservation practices, given their dependence on local ecosystems. While this appears to be true of many, it cannot be generalized to all. Johannes (1981) and Klee (1980) give examples from the Pacific islands, where this assumption appears to be satisfied. Rudge (1986), however, points out that the practices of the Maori did not always result in the preservation of species (e.g., the moa) nor in the conservation of natural habitats (e.g., their use of fire may have altered vegetation). The Maoris were responsible, it seems, for hunting the large flightless moa to extinction. It has also been suggested that aborigines in Australia considerably modified the natural environment by the use of fire and other means and were responsible for the extinction of some giant marsupial species. Blainey (1976), after reviewing the evidence, suggests that the arrival of Australian aborigines and their weapons and firesticks played a major role in the extinction of species and in change in vegetation. He claims that "certainly there is no justification for the assumption—widespread in the 1970s—that the aboriginals lived in complete harmony with the natural environment" (Blainey, 1976, p. 58). The idea of conserving species for the sake of doing so has also been said to be absent or to be a low preference in some traditional societies, such as Africa.

Not all early societies had a stronger conservation ethic than those in developed Western countries. Indeed, it is likely that some had more barbaric attitudes as invaders of "new" lands, such as prehistoric settlers in the Americas. But the state of technology and organization of early societies was such as to limit severely their power over nature compared with that of modern societies. Hence, even in cases where there was little respect for nature and desire to sustain natural environments, the actual power of traditional people was often inadequate to bring about a major change. It is possible to overdraw the image of Rousseau's "noble savage" intent on conserving nature, although it does seem that many traditional societies did have well-developed conservation codes and practices. But it is now very difficult for those traditional societies with positive conservation codes and practices to maintain these in the face of economic growth, development, and change.

POPULATION GROWTH AND ECONOMIC GROWTH

Neo-Malthusians have tended to emphasize population growth and growing aggregate production in LDCs as a major threat to the conservation of resources in developing countries. Such growth leads to the destruction of natural environments and to greater human competition with nature. Demand from developed countries for exports of natural resources from LDCs to support their economic growth and their high living standards is also seen as a further contributor to the natural resource depletion in LDCs. While these factors are not unimportant, attention should be given in addition to other developments that increase the difficulties of conserving resources in LDCs, including the growth of markets and the market system, the rapidity of technological change (the availability of new technology), and the development of institutions that have undermined local authority, responsibility, and concern.

DEVELOPMENT OF THE MARKET SYSTEM

Introduction or improvement in the operation of the market system of exchange is often seen as an important element in the development process. While the market system can have advantages for economic efficiency, it can have drawbacks from a conservation viewpoint. Individual self-interest is the linchpin of the system, and the system develops by encouraging this motive. In so doing, it may weaken systems of social responsibility in relation to exploitation of the environment.

The extension of the market often means that purchasers or users of a product are remote from the place of production or origin of the product and feel no social responsibility for any environmental damage caused by its production (see Chapter 2). The market system is impersonal, the information of participants about the effects of its operation is limited, and in many cases participants have no incentive to collect more complete information.

When markets come into existence, market failures, such as externalities, may occur. LDCs in which traditional institutions have been undermined are often in a weak position to correct for such failures. Furthermore, while strong legislation may exist in support of conservation, lack of resources for policing and the presence of bribery can easily make such laws ineffective. Inadequate resources may be available to enforce regulations.

In addition, urban bias—that is, resource and economic policies designed to favor urban dwellers—and failure to take account of nontraded goods may occur. This is well illustrated by the study of Julian Caldecott and Adrian Nyaoi (1985) in Sarawak of the felling of rainforest for timber. Although strong urban pressures exist for the felling of such rainforest, Caldecott was able to show that its preservation is of considerable value to the Daiyak people in providing subsistence supplies of meat—that is, the rainforest provides food (berries, nuts, etc.) for wild pigs, which, in turn, are a valuable food source. Even economists have tended to ignore the loss of the gathering and hunting component with agricultural development. Most studies of the Green Revolution, for example, tend to ignore the reduced access of the very poor to natural resources such as thatch, fuel, and water (Alauddin & Tisdell, 1989). Thus among economists there tends to be a market bias— that is, a bias toward taking into account only marketed or traded commodities.

RAPID TECHNOLOGICAL CHANGE

Many traditional communities have been faced with rapid technological change and have not been able to alter their customs and practices quickly enough to adjust to these. Species and living resources that were safe from overexploitation with traditional techniques are no longer safe. Many examples could be cited, including:

1. the overexploitation of dugong in the Torres Strait with the introduction of boats having outboard motors, which means that dugong can easily be pursued and harpooned (Tisdell, 1986);

2. accelerated reduction in turtle populations following the greater use of boats with outboard motors: relatively remote islands can now be easily reached by hunters, and pursuit of turtles is easier (Tisdell, 1986);

3. the serious reduction in populations of birds-of-paradise in Papua New Guinea, where the feathers of these birds are in considerable demand for use as adornment, with the introduction of guns;

4. similarly, a number of bird species were highly valued for their plumes by the Polynesians in Hawaii, and after European contact and the introduction of guns, they hunted several of these species to extinction (Day, 1981).

New technologies can also lead to the more rapid clearing of natural habitat for agriculture and for intensive economic pursuits, as well as to the release of pollutants that may be harmful to nature. Very often habitat modification and environmental change are more powerful forces than increased hunting pressure in bringing about the extinction of species.

New technology itself may play a major role in the extension of the market by allowing goods to be exchanged over greater distances. In the case of the dugong, for example, the introduction of outboard motors and refrigeration made it possible for some villages in the Torres Strait to market their dugong in Daru, a sizable town, rather than distribute dugong in the customary manner in the village. The availability of this market provided a source of cash income and resulted in increased pressure being placed on dugong stocks (Tisdell, 1986).

NEW INSTITUTIONS UNDERMINING LOCAL CONCERN ABOUT AND CONTROL OVER THE ENVIRONMENT

As pointed out earlier, development of the market system tends to undermine local control over and concern about the local environment. This is so even when the system only involves the exchange of goods, for in this case economic production becomes impersonalized, and knowledge of productive activities is limited. But if the market system adds to labor mobility of people, as seems likely, it may further weaken incentives to conserve local resources, that is, to sustain local production and environments. Given mobility, it is possible for individuals to move elsewhere, hopefully to less degraded environments, if they degrade their local environment. Thus there is less incentive to adopt productive systems that are locally sustainable.

The emergence of nation states with relatively centralized administration is another factor weakening local control over and direct concern about the local environment. In many cases ownership and control over local living resources has been taken from local communities and placed in the hands of government departments that have little or no representation at the local level. Traditional means of control over the exploitation of local resources are weakened and not replaced by effective central government control. For instance, Jefferies (1982) has observed this in relation to the Himalayas in Nepal; when the regulation of forests was taken out of the hands of local communities and vested in the Forestry Department with its headquarters in Katmandu, effective control over the cutting of timber for fuel in the Himalayas was lost. Other cases could also be cited.

In addition, the imposition of taxes on villagers by central governments may lead to greater pressure on living resources. Villages may try to exploit these more heavily to obtain cash to pay their taxes. This has been said to add to pressure on the dugong in the Torres Strait (Tisdell, 1986).

Institutional arrangements that allow owners or managers of resources not to reside in local areas where these resources are being exploited may result in little responsibility being felt for the environmental impact of their use. Furthermore, little concern may be shown about the sustainability of the local community and the sustainability of local production. The managers of public companies and multinational enterprises are often engaged in the management of resources geographically distant from their residence or community, if they have a sense of community.

The rise of public companies has implications for resource conservation in LDCs as multinational companies sometimes operate in LDCs, and LDCs have their own public companies, particularly in their modern sector. In large public companies, managers and owners tend to be separated. The separation of ownership and management in large companies has, it has been suggested, left managers with considerable discretion about the aims which can be pursued in running a company (Berle & Means, 1932). This means that even if shareholders happened to be concerned about the environmental impact of a company's operations either in their own country or abroad, say in a developing country, they may have little power to counteract it. But even shareholders with large holdings and possible influence, such as large insurance companies, may be unconcerned about the environmental spillovers from a company's operation if the spillovers enable the company to earn greater profit than otherwise. Furthermore, they may argue that if they do not take advantage of the situation others who are less scrupulous will, and will gladly buy their shares.

Within a large company, top managers are often located at considerable distance from the unpleasant production activities of their company. For example, the top managers of BHP (an Australian multinational company) are located in Australia, very far away from their Ok Tedi gold and copper mine in Papua New

Guinea. One expects them to be less concerned with environmental consequences than if they lived in the immediate vicinity. The majority of beneficiaries in the government of Papua New Guinea are in a similar position. The fact that this mining operation is causing considerable sedimentation in the Fly River and may be leading to a build-up of heavy metals may be of little concern to them.

Even given the proposition that shareholders have little influence over managers, profit and company growth may still be important to managers, either on the basis of growth by internal funding, as suggested by Penrose (1959), or because of the discipline imposed by the possibility of financial take-over of a nonprofit maximizing firm, as suggested by Marris (1964). A public company that fails to maximize returns from the economic opportunities that it has (including possible adverse exploitation of the environment) risks being the subject of a financial take-over or raid. Such factors may result in companies neglecting environmental spillovers, both at home and abroad.

Furthermore, the growing practice of sharing responsibility via committee decision-making (whether within firms or government) may mean that no individual feels a particular personal responsibility for the adverse environmental consequences of any collective decision made. Such impersonal economic institutional arrangements characteristic of developed countries are being increasingly adopted by LDCs.

SOME ADDITIONAL REASONS
FOR LACK OF CONSERVATION IN LDCs

Several other factors are inimical to resource conservation in LDCs, even though ecosystem people in LDCs may have a strong desire for ecological and economic sustainability. High rates of interest in developing countries and pressing current needs are sometimes seen as factors contributing to rapid depletion of resources in LDCs, and those individuals near starvation may grasp at straws. But against this must be set the desire for sustainability of production, which is reinforced by low rates of labor and population mobility in LDCs and the limited operation of markets.

Foreign investors in LDCs, on the other hand, may apply high discount rates to projects if they feel that governments in LDCs are politically unstable. This means that the resources are exploited more rapidly than otherwise. Speed of depletion of resources rather than sustainability thus becomes a prime consideration.

Such factors as corruption, lack of law and order, and the unavailability of effective enforcement of technology and the possible *dominance* of pro-economic growth groups may compound the difficulties faced by LDCs in conserving living resources. The consolidation of national control over natural resources in LDCs, as has occurred in many of the new nation states, may make these resources more vulnerable to exploitation by political and economic elites for their own advantage and may not promote the general welfare of society, nor a proconservation stance. The social structure of LDCs in transition may encourage resource exploitation by elites, as suggested by Hoogvelt (1978, p. 137).

Many rural dwellers see greater central government control over their natural resources as a means of exploitation by urban elites who are often out of contact with the vital ecological role that such resources play in the lives of rural people. Movements such as the Chipko movement—the movement to hug trees—in India are a response to such developments. In discussing this movement, Sinha (1984, p. 183) comments:

The villagers have also seen how successive Governments have taken away their forest wealth and turned it into a resource bank for faraway urban markets. Even for minor forest produce and articles of daily necessity like firewood, the local people have been forced to become thieves in their homeland.

INTERESTS OF DEVELOPED COUNTRIES IN CONSERVATION IN LDCs

As mentioned earlier, developed countries have a variety of interests in encouraging conservation in LDCs. They may act out of self-interest as well as for altruistic reasons, or both.

Some of the possible benefits that developed countries may obtain from nature conservation in less developed countries are:

1. existence, option, and bequest values from living resources conservation even though the population of developed countries is clearly not resident in LDCs—residents of LDCs may, for example, be pleased to know that pandas continue to exist in the wild in China, to have the option kept open of seeing them there, and many also gain satisfaction from the knowledge that their descendants will be able to see these animals in the wild;

2. sustainability of supplies of raw materials or sustainability at a lower price;

3. consumer surpluses obtained by tourists from developed countries, who visit LDCs to see the type of nature conserved;

4. maintenance of gene banks that help to keep options open for future possible uses of living resources, for example, for food and for medicine, and which also reduce the risk of the collapse of presently cultivated varieties of crops in developed countries;

5. to the extent that the "greenhouse effect" is important and the removal of forests in LDCs adds to this effect, conserving forests in LDCs will benefit developed countries; however, it would appear that the major contributor to rising carbon dioxide levels in the atmosphere is the burning of large quantities of fossil fuel in developed countries rather than the removal of trees in LDCs;

6. where a developed country is directly exploiting a migratory stock such as a fish stock that breeds in a less developed country, it will have a direct interest in conservation measures there—for example, southern bluefin tuna breed off the southwest of Indonesia in the Indian Ocean, then migrate toward Australia and into the southern Indian Ocean, where they are caught by Australian, Japanese, and New Zealand fishing boats; any action by Indonesia that might threaten the breeding of southern bluefin tuna would adversely affect three developed countries—Australia, Japan, and New Zealand—and so they have an interest in conservation in the Indonesian marine area;

7. in relation to aid to LDCs, developed countries may have a particular interest in ensuring that supported projects are ecologically viable and sustainable, according to the *World Conservation Strategy*, in encouraging sustainable development, otherwise foreign aid may prove ineffective, or rising amounts of aid may be required to maintain a living standard target; a number of aid agencies—e.g., USAID—have now started to take into account the environmental impact of projects, and so has the World Bank.

The above points raise the question of who should pay for conservation in LDCs. Even if the principle of he-who-benefits ought to pay is adopted, it is inappropriate to generalize about this matter—for example, to claim that developed countries should always pay. Some conservation projects may exclusively benefit an LDC, others may be of considerable joint benefit to an LDC and developed countries, still others may primarily benefit developed countries.

Developed countries may be in a comparatively weak position to place moral pressure on LDCs to engage in more conservation, for two reasons: not all developing countries subscribe to nature conservation ethics, and it is difficult to put moral pressure on those who do not share common ethics; secondly, developed countries in their earlier phases of growth often showed little regard for conservation of species. Consequently, LDCs may respond to requests from developing countries for more conservation effort by pointing out that they are being asked to adopt behaviour that developed countries were incapable of or unwilling to adopt in their earlier economic growth phase. On the other hand, the penalties now for not paying adequate attention to conservation may be greater than in the past, since LDCs do not have access to the new frontiers with seemingly unlimited natural resources that today's developed countries had during their own "age of expansion." Nevertheless, unless LDCs perceive a net benefit to themselves from extra conservation effort or unless they are adequately compensated by developed countries for this, it is idle to expect them to make an extra sacrifice to conserve living resources on the basis that developed countries see virtue in this. Some theory about the distribution of gains from conservation in LDCs can throw more light on the issues involved.

THEORY OF PUBLIC GOODS AND
INTERNATIONAL SPILLOVER OF BENEFITS FROM
CONSERVATION IN LDCs

Consider the relevance of the theory of public goods (Brown & Jackson, 1986) to international spillover of benefits from conservation in LDCs and the theory's relevance to international policy intended to foster conservation in LDCs. In this respect consider Figure 4.1: suppose that curve ABD or function $Y = g(X)$ represents the marginal benefit to an LDC of conservation in it and that curve EFG or $Y = t(X)$ indicates the marginal benefit to the whole

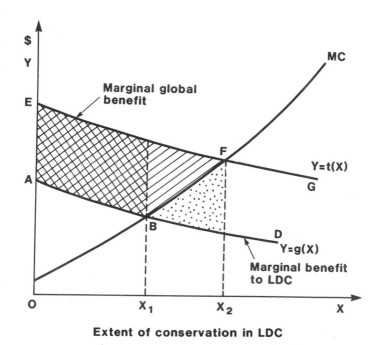

Figure 4.1 International spillover benefits from conservation in a less developed country as illustrated by the theory of public goods.

world of this conservation. The difference between these two curves represents the marginal spillover benefits to the rest of the world. Let the curve identified by MC represent the marginal cost of conservation in the LDC.

In the absence of appropriation of spillover benefits the LDC will find it optimal to provide for conservation only to the extent X_1, for at this point the LDC's marginal benefit from conservation equals its marginal cost. At this level of conservation the rest of the world obtains a spillover benefit of

$$\int_0^{X_1} t(X)\, dX - \int_0^{X_1} g(X)\, dX$$

(shown by the cross-hatched area), but the extent of conservation is insufficient to maximize global economic benefits. Conservation on a scale X_2 is required for this purpose, for at this scale global marginal benefits from conservation in the LDC equal the marginal cost of such conservation. But unless the rest of the world at least transfers an amount indicated by the dotted area to the LDC, it will have no incentive to engage in an optimal amount of conservation. A bargaining problem may emerge: the LDC may try to obtain the dotted *plus* the hatched area in any negotiation aimed at increasing its level of conservation from X_1 to X_2. This area represents the maximum amount the rest of the world would be prepared to pay for this additional amount of conservation.

Especially if most of the spillover gains go to more developed countries, the LDC may try to put moral pressure on developed countries to obtain a transfer for itself equal to the cross-hatched area plus the hatched and dotted areas. If developed countries were to transfer this sum, they would be left with no net benefit from conservation in the LDC. Thus an income distribution issue is raised as well as a potential bargaining problem involving a sum equal to the dotted area in Figure 4.1 as a minimum transfer for optimality and the dotted plus hatched area as the maximum transfer from developed countries.

However, a free-riding problem may also exist in the rest of the world. If a number of countries benefit from conservation in the LDC, each may try to ride free on the other in relation to aid for conservation in the LDC, and in the end the largest gainer may contribute more than proportionately to its gain. Unfortunately, because of free-riding an optimal outcome is not assured, and the amount of conservation in the LDC may be inadequate from a global standpoint.

An LDC may, of course, by adopting particular policies, appropriate some of the benefits of its conservation, which would otherwise spill over to other countries. The *World Conservation Strategy* (IUCN, 1980) advocates that LDCs try to appropriate a greater fraction of gains, for example, by charges on foreign tourists making use of the conserved natural resources of LDCs. But even if this is done to the optimal extent possible, international spillovers can be expected to persist. This could be illustrated by drawing a curve intermediate between ABD and EFG, representing domestic direct marginal benefits to the LDC plus benefits "clawed back" from foreigners. The greater the extent to which marginal benefits are clawed back from foreigners, the greater is the scope the LDC has for profitably expanding conservation.

Because developed countries can benefit from greater conservation in LDCs, they may adopt policies to support such conservation. A variety of possible economic policies that may assist in this regard are outlined in Chapter 3 on "The Role of the International Economy" in *Our Common Future* (World Commission on Environment and Development, 1987). Apart from providing direct aid and foreign debt forgiveness for conservation in an LDC and giving particular attention to conservation aspects in foreign aid that is not primarily conservation-related, developed countries may adopt other strategies to promote conservation in LDCs.

An LDC may, for example, be failing to achieve an optimal level of conservation from its own point of view because of defective organization or absence of motivation in the LDC in favor of conservation. In relation to Figure 4.1, its amount of conservation may be less than X_1. Developed countries may assist in improving administrative organization and influence the main power groups to be more favorably disposed to conservation. Political stability and law and order are, of course, necessary to achieve any conservation goals of significance. In some LDCs, civil war and conflict make it extremely difficult or impossible to achieve even minimal conservation goals.

In some cases, LDCs may underestimate their benefits from conservation. This means, in relation to Figure 4.1, that their perceived marginal benefit curve is below their actual one. Developed countries may be able to counteract this by providing information to show LDCs their actual estimated benefits and so expand the extent of their conservation effort, thereby indirectly providing benefits to developed countries.

INTERNAL INCOME DISTRIBUTION, VARIABILITY, AND SUSTAINABILITY CONSEQUENCES OF CONSERVATION IN LDCs

A dimension of conservation that requires particular attention is its impact on income distribution in LDCs. Not all conservation projects have a favorable impact on income distribution within

LDCs, although many do. In this respect, experience with (a) the Amboseli National Park and the Masai people in Kenya (Western, 1982) and (b) Chitwan National Park and the local people in Nepal (Mishra, 1982) can be quoted.

The Amboseli National Park in Kenya was established in an area traditionally used by the Masai people. They were initially opposed to it and resisted it, for example, by poaching, as they were denied the use of resources traditionally used by them such as access to water for cattle and access to game. Originally most of those employed in the Park were not Masai, and most of the income received from the Park was transferred to the central government in Nairobi. Given the resistance of the Masai, the policy was modified to increase the extent of their employment in park administration, to provide outlets for the sale of their handicrafts through the Park, and to pipe water from the Park so as to provide supplies of water for their cattle during drought periods.

The Chitwan National Park in Nepal was established for the main purpose of protecting the tiger. Villagers resident within its boundaries were relocated outside the Park and denied access to resources in it. Their economic circumstances deteriorated as a result, and none were employed in the administration of the Park. In addition, they were sometimes harassed by animals from the Park, such as marauding tigers. In order to alleviate their economic situation, they are now allowed at particular times of the year to collect grass in the Park for thatch and fallen timber for firewood.

On the other hand, examples of conservation projects that have relatively favored the poor, such as those controlling deforestation, could also be quoted.

Apart from the productivity enhancing or reducing the impact of conservation and its influences on income distribution, particular attention may need to be given to its impact on the variability of benefits and on income security. Lack of conservation may result in more variable environmental conditions, such as greater extremes in the volume of river flows. It may also lead to the loss of natural resource reserves that play a valuable role in social security for the very poor in rural society, such as the landless poor, who may be more reliant on hunting and gathering activities, and for village communities, for example their use of forest areas in Papua New Guinea Highlands, as mentioned by Clarke (1971). Possibilities of drawing on natural resources to supplement their needs may be extremely important for the rural poor. This is especially so in difficult economic times, for these resources act as reserves to draw on, much as accumulated cash balances or savings function in monetary economies. Economists often fail to take account of the multidimensional nature of welfare, which is influenced not only by income levels but by security, stability, and sustainability of income (cf. Conway, 1987; Tisdell, 1988b).

CONCLUDING COMMENTS

In considering development issues in LDCs, economists have in the past given little attention to conservation, especially living resource conservation; possibly they continue to do so. But in this regard they risk being out of contact with the concerns of a substantial group in contemporary society.

Randall (1986) states that economists live high in the "information food chain." In addition, it could be added, they live high on the "social-policy-making chain." What they choose to take into account in their models can, therefore, have important policy and social consequences. For example, the types of productivity relationships they choose to adopt or ignore will influence their policy recommendations. When leading economists I. M. D. Little and J. A. Mirrlees (1974) expressed the view that externalities were relatively unimportant in LDCs—they established a "presumption" that they might reasonably be ignored. But interdependence between living things is important in developing countries, and environmental externalities or spillovers can be very important.

This was graphically brought home to me in 1987, when I visited the island of Los Negros in the Philippines. Along the coast north of Dumaguete are fishing villages where some very poor fishermen live. The abundance of fish in these areas has been adversely affected by the enclosure of marshlands and wetlands (estuarine breeding areas for fish and other marine organisms) for prawn farming. Not only are these areas effectively separated from the sea, but mangroves are destroyed in the process. Replenishment of fish and crustacean populations near the fishing villages is adversely affected, and less organic matter is available to marine organisms, thus reducing the natural productivity of the marine area. Furthermore, prawn farming is a capital-intensive, low labor-intensity enterprise. Thus the incomes of already very poor fishermen have been further reduced.

The World Bank is involved in the Central Visayas project in Los Negros. One module of this project involves the replanting of mangroves, the provision of artificial reefs and of small marine reserves (breeding grounds under village control), and the restocking of areas with giant clams. Such measures have been shown by researchers at the University of Dumaguete to have a major impact in increasing fish production and thus helping to reduce the poverty of coastal village dwellers.

Environmental and ecological interdependence must not be ignored in evaluating economic projects in less developed countries since these factors can have major consequences for the level, distribution, variability, and sustainability of income.

Nature conservation in LDCs involves a diversity of issues. Concern about it is not misplaced, given strong economic pressures for change and growth in LDCs. Policy responses are required both at the macro- and the micro-level, as illustrated here. The welfare both of the less developed as well as the developed world is potentially at stake.

5

Energy Resources and Depletable
Resources as Limits to Growth:
Optimists versus Pessimists

As economic growth has proceeded, people have become
increasingly dependent on nonrenewable or depletable resources,
especially nonrenewable energy resources such as coal, oil, and
natural gas, which represent an increasing proportion of consumption and to a large extent make possible the economic growth of the
Western world (Maitra, 1988a, 1988b; Podder, 1988). Without
access to such resources, the Industrial Revolution would not have
proceeded very far, for it would have been tied to human and
animal power and to wood as its main source of fuel.

Toward the end of the 1960s and especially during the early
1970s, as oil prices began to rise, there was increased concern that
economic growth experienced in the Western world would not
prove sustainable because of growing shortages of nonrenewable
resources especially fossil fuels such as coal, oil, and natural gas.
Indeed, the more pessimistic predicted impending economic collapse as a result of limits to growth set by the finite availability of
such resources, unless the exponentially growing demands on natural resources by man were significantly reduced. The Club of
Rome, for example (Meadows et al., 1972), warned (as pointed out
by Lecomber, 1979, p. 7) that if consumption rates continue to grow

as they are, present reserves of most minerals will be exhausted within 50 years and "the breakdown of society and the irreversible disruption of life support systems on this planet are inevitable." In the absence of changed behavior on the part of man, such a breakdown is therefore predicted to occur around the year 2020.

Pessimists, while they may differ in their relative emphasis, basically see resource depletion and pollution as preventing unlimited economic growth. They believe that:

1. the world's reserves of non-renewable energy and other resources will be depleted, or almost so, within a few decades, thereby causing an economic crisis; and/or

2. global pollution from resource-use will be so damaging that a sudden halt to economic growth and a substantial reduction in economic production will occur. Global pollution due to burning of fossil fuels may result in rising carbon dioxide levels and be responsible for the "greenhouse effect" (the warming of the Earth's atmosphere). Hence, it could lead to a melting of the ice-caps and a substantial rise of sea levels and to major climatic changes.

But there are other areas of concern, including acid rains and radiation hazards from nuclear power generation.

BASIC PESSIMISTIC MODELS

One of the most basic pessimistic models of limits to economic growth is that expounded by the Club of Rome (Meadows et al., 1972). It assumes that economic growth will proceed at a constant percentage rate and that this growing output will require non-renewable resources in approximately fixed proportions. However, stocks of nonrenewable resources have an upper limit, as indicated by reserves of these, for example, reserves of oil. Once stocks of these nonrenewable resources are used up, a decline (a disastrous decline) in production is inevitable.

For simplicity, suppose that all production is achieved by using one nonrenewable resource—say, oil—required in given proportions. Let OS represent the available reserves of "oil" in the base period, as indicated in Figure 5.1. If growth in output (compared to the base) occurs at a constant percentage rate so that annual output follows path OCD. cumulated output from the base period follows

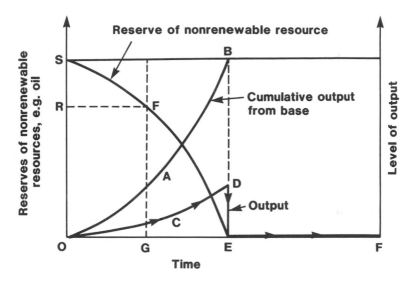

Figure 5.1 A stylized illustration of the Club of Rome's model of depletion of nonrenewable resources due to the growth of economic production.

curve OAB, and the remaining level of stocks of the nonrenewable resource follows the curve SFE, then by the end of the period of time, OE, total reserves of the renewable resource are exhausted and production comes to a halt. This sudden economic calamity occurs since no output is available to support the population, if remaining renewable resources are of little consequence. Indeed unless it changes its ways, the human species seems to be ultimately doomed. Meadows et al. (1972) warn that this calamity may approach unexpectedly, given the exponential nature of growth; for example, halfway through the period to economic collapse (at time G), reserves of the nonrenewable resource still appear to be quite large because only a small fraction of reserves, SR, have been depleted. Thus many individuals will have no hint of the imminence of resource exhaustion and economic collapse.

This is, of course, a highly stylized version of the Club of Rome scenario of growth prospects. In addition, they warn that there are limits to the Earth's ability to absorb pollutants from production—that is, to act as a sink for pollutants. Environmental pollution is viewed as a by-product of economic production. Once accumulated pollutants in the environment exceed a threshold, this may have catastrophic environmental effects. For example, rising carbon dioxide levels, and the greenhouse effect generally, may set in train the melting of the polar ice-caps. Once the triggering has occurred—that is, once the existing environmental equilibrium has been sufficiently disturbed—the process of environmental change may be irreversible. The occurrence of major environmental dislocation can be expected to cause a collapse in economic production. Either resource depletion or exhaustion of the environment's capacity to absorb wastes or pollutants without major environmental dislocation will limit economic growth soon in the view of the Club of Rome because of growth limits or barriers.

These prospects have led to several policy recommendations to curb growing demands on the Earth's limited nonrenewable resources. A number of individuals (Ehrlich & Harriman, 1971; Daly, 1980) advocate a steady-state or stationary economy as ideal. This is one in which use of resources remains stationary, and so exponential growth is avoided.

The policy recommendations of Daly (1980) are representative of a large group of growth pessimists. He recommends:

1. zero population growth;

2. restrained consumption per capita—desirably held to a *minimum* tolerable level per head.

In addition, he recommends that quotas be imposed by governments on the annual use of nonrenewable resources, e.g., fossil fuels, and that quota rights be auctioned so as to promote economic efficiency. If markets are competitive, markets in and transferability of quota rights should promote economic efficiency in any period of time relative to the aggregate amount of nonrenewable resources permitted to be used. Daly sees the benefit of such an approach as being one of permitting the human species to survive as long as possible or, at least, as long as is compatible, in his view, with God's wish. In his opinion, the longest possible period of survival of the human species should be the major goal of mankind.

While it is true that a steady-state world economy would significantly extend the period required for depletion of nonrenewable resources, this steady state may not be sustainable in perpetuity, given current world population levels. Georgescu-Roegen (1975) has argued that zero population growth and a steady-state world economy at current levels is not sustainable in perpetuity. It will lead to resource exhaustion in a finite period. This period can be extended by reducing population levels and the aggregate level of economic activity, but he is pessimistic about the possibility of *ultimately* being able to avoid nonrenewable resource exhaustion. He argues this on the basis of the fundamental laws of physics. Nonrenewable resources, when used, tend to be irretrievably dissipated. This follows from the Second Law of Thermodynamics, also known as the Law of Entropy, which states that the entropy, spread, or disorder of a closed heat-energy system continuously increases. Any biological or economic activity results in greater dissipation of energy, and eventually all energy resources become so dissipated that man can no longer use them. Matter, too, is subject to irrevocable dissipation. In Georgescu-Roegen's (1971) view while technological progress can defer the date of complete dissipation or depletion of nonrenewable resources, it cannot prevent their ultimate depletion as a result of their continuing use in economic activity.

Indeed, Georgescu-Roegen states quite emphatically that the world's population must be reduced to a level that can be fed by organic agriculture alone. He emphasizes that "to set a higher level by counting on mechanized agriculture and heavy-feeding high-yielding varieties means to turn one's back to the present handwriting on the wall" (Georgescu-Roegen, 1976, p. xviii).

Major philosophical issues, especially concerning values, are raised once it has been accepted that there are finite possibilities for nonrenewable resource use. What, for instance, is the optimal distribution of human population over time, and how should inter-generational competition for nonrenewable resource use be settled (Tisdell, 1988)? Some indication of the possible alternative paths and choices can be seen from Figure 5.2.

One possibility is to continue on an exponential path of population and income growth, as indicated by Path (1) in Figure 5.2, which then results in collapse and possibly the early extinction of the human species. The future existence of the species may then be "short but exciting." Path (2) is a steady state at existing population levels and aggregate levels of economic activity. This much extends

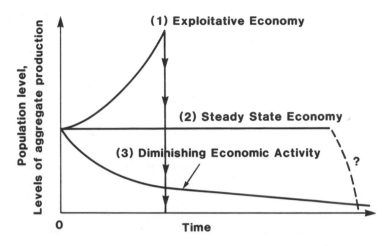

Figure 5.2 Alternative possible global population and economic growth scenarios, given nonrenewable resource and environmental limits to growth.

the length of survival of the human species but may not completely remove the spectre of resource exhaustion. Thirdly, population levels and levels of economic activity may be reduced over time, so extending the period of survival of the human species tremendously (maybe without limit), as indicated by Path (3).

CRITICISM OF THE PESSIMISTIC POSITION

Criticism of the pessimistic prognosis can be listed as follows:

1. *Population growth.* Projections of population growth based on exponential growth are naive. As income rises, population growth tends to taper off and may become zero or negative, as experience in developed countries seems to indicate. Nevertheless, this still leaves open the threat from greater resource-use due to rising levels of per capita consumption.

2. *Reserves of nonrenewable resources.* Official estimates of reserves of nonrenewable resources as used by the Club of Rome (Meadows, et al., 1972) are claimed to be gross underestimates of

available reserves. Companies only prove reserves a limited period ahead of their use, since costs are involved in proving reserves. Also, several areas of the Earth are as yet imperfectly explored for nonrenewable resources, and the reserves that these hold are not included in estimates. Furthermore, officially stated reserves are usually reserves that it is economic to exploit, given current prices and technology. Marginal, submarginal, and latent reserves are present as a rule and often are very large. Indeed, the quantity of economic reserves of a resource can normally be expressed as a rising function of the price paid for it (see Tisdell, 1982).

However, resource pessimists argue that given their assumption of *exponential* growth, a multiple increase (e.g., a quadrupling) in the world's finite available resources will not significantly extend the period of time required to exhaust nonrenewable resources. Given the logic of exponential resource depletion, the amount of time required for ultimate exhaustion of resources is little extended (cf. Lecomber, 1979, pp. 14–15).

3. *Technological change.*   The pessimistic position has been criticized on the grounds that it does not give sufficient weight to the possibility (likelihood) that continuing technological progress will counteract or more than counteract the limitations posed by finite nonrenewable resource availability.

Club of Rome adherents point out that if technological progress is allowed for by raising notional levels of reserves of nonrenewable resources, then this will not extend their usable life by much, given the logic of exponential resource depletion. On the other hand, the technological optimists predict that technological progress will proceed in an exponential fashion and be capable of overcoming limitations. Georgescu-Roegen (1971) argues on theoretical grounds that no degree of ingenuity by man can ultimately prevent the depletion of nonrenewable energy resources because of physical principles of entropy.

4. *Price mechanism.*   According to critics, growth pessimists fail to take adequately into account the ability of the price mechanism to ration and conserve resources over time. As a resource becomes scarce, its price will rise, and among other things its use will be economized. Given the price mechanism, there is no need

for governments to restrict the use of nonrenewable resources by direct intervention, since conservation will automatically come about as a result of the operation of individual self-interest.

5. *Resource substitution.* The scope for resource substitution is claimed to be much greater than is supposed by growth pessimists (Hartley & Tisdell, 1981, Chapter 13). Hence, economic growth is not as narrowly tied to the availability of particular resources such as those of nonrenewable energy, as the pessimists suppose. Because a considerable amount of resource substitution is possible, the depletion of a particular nonrenewable resource may be of little consequence for the continuance of the economic growth. Even nonenergy resources, such as insulation or the greater use of electronic communication rather than actual travel, can substitute for use of energy.

6. *Signaling of impending resource exhaustion.* The view of some pessimists that resource exhaustion may occur without warning is challenged by a number of economists. They argue that impending resource exhaustion will be signaled by a rise in price of an input that is falling in availability, and this will automatically lead to its reduced use and increased conservation. But some pessimists argue that the price mechanism may not work well because producers overestimate the potential for technological progress and the price mechanism has little impact on trends in aggregates such as population growth and the growth in aggregate production.

OPTIMISTIC VIEWS AND PREDICTIONS ABOUT ECONOMIC GROWTH AND NATURAL RESOURCE AVAILABILITY

Optimistic views of the possibilities for continuing economic growth usually suppose that the power of technological progress to overcome resource constraints is virtually unlimited. In addition, some emphasize that available nonrenewable resources are extremely large (virtually infinite) and that feedback mechanisms will come into play to prevent human self-extinction if this is a real possibility. Furthermore, the scope for substituting resources and using backstop technologies is so great that we need have no worry from a scarcity point of view about the exhaustion of particular nonrenewable resources such as oil. In addition, some growth optimists project past trends into the future to support their case.

Although they did not build a formal model, Kahn, Brown, and Martel (1976) argue that the most reasonable assumption for economic growth is that it will follow an S-shaped logistic curve for the main components (population levels, GDP, and per capita income) in the absence of any public intervention. World population, gross product, and per capita income will continue to rise for the next 200 years or so and then stabilize. During this period, the world's population will more than triple, gross production will be increased 85-fold, and average per capita income will go up more than 15-fold. New technologies, better use of existing resources including wastes, and greater use of energy resources other than oil will help to make this possible. Greater use can be made of coal, both directly and indirectly through liquefication (coal resources are still vast). More use can be made of very vast shale oil deposits, nuclear power (fission in the short term and fusion in the long term), and alternative "soft" energy sources such as solar technologies.

Kahn et al. (1976) point out that in the last 200 years or so there has been a great increase in world population, production, and per capita income. They are optimistic that new technology will permit the process to continue for another 200 years or so and that as incomes rise in less developed countries, their populations will stabilize in the same way as has happened in the Western world (Tietenberg, 1988). Their perspective is illustrated in a generalized fashion in Figure 5.3.

The Kahn et al. (1976) scenarios make use of most of the optimistic assumptions mentioned above, such as the rapid increase in technological progress, and a self-regulating population, that is, stabilization of population levels. It might, however, be pointed out here that "superoptimists" such as Julian Simon (1977) do not see continual population growth as a constraint or a barrier to economic growth. They argue that people are the ultimate resource, and a greater population will mean more ideas and even greater technological progress. Far from rising human populations being a barrier to growth and an economic problem, they are an economic asset.

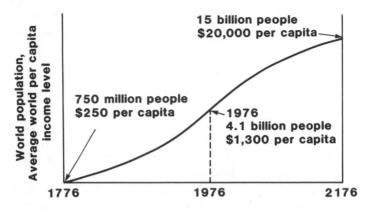

Figure 5.3 Illustration of the generalized perspective of Kahn et al. (1976) on world growth prospects. Note that fixed 1975 dollar values are used.

Undoubtedly, a key element in the optimistic position is technological optimism. Lecomber (1979, p. 28) points out that while elaborate models may sometimes obscure the basic difference between growth optimists and pessimists, the basic position is clear:

Optimists believe that technical progress and substitutions of man-made for natural resources will outweigh the increasing relative physical scarcity of resources as they undoubtedly seem to have in the past. By contrast, pessimists foresee, or at least fear, the eventual failure of technical progress, the advent of problems for which solutions cannot be found or are not found in time.

Optimists believe that technological progress will overcome in practice any tendency towards decreasing returns. This is illustrated by the theories of Barnett and Morse (1963, p. 236):

A strong case can be made for the view that the accumulation of knowledge and technical progress is automatic and self-reproductive in modern economies and obeys a law of increasing returns. Every cost-reducing innovation opens up new possibilities of application in so many new directions that the stock of knowledge, far from being depleted by new developments, may even expand geometrically.

Note the following sources of optimism: (1) the process of expansion of technical knowledge is automatic and self-reproductive; (2) the stock of knowledge expands exponentially, and (3) the result is increasing returns to effort.

In support of their views, Barnett and Morse (1963) examined trends in the costs of extracting minerals, fuels, and other raw materials in the United States between 1900 and 1957. They found the general trend to be downwards. Baumol and Oates (1979) updated the analysis to cover the period from 1900 to 1975 and obtained a similar downward trend in terms of real per unit costs of extraction. The falling secular trend is indicative of the ability of technological progress to more than offset any increase in extraction costs, which might otherwise occur as superior natural resources are mined first. On the basis of their empirical evidence, Barnett and Morse reject the view that the real cost of the extractive output will increase over time in a growing economy.

Margaret Slade (1982), on the other hand, produces evidence that calls for less optimism. She found that the trends of the real prices of the 12 mineral commodities she examined are best approximated by U-shaped quadratic curves. Furthermore, she observed that the price of every mineral had passed the minimum point on its U-shaped curve by 1978. If the current trend, therefore, were to continue as identified by Slade, we could expect the real prices of minerals to rise despite technological progress. Thus increasing scarcity is being signaled (or, alternatively, there is more monopoly power in resource markets), and this may exert a drag on economic growth. Certainly, it seems that the degree of optimism suggested by the empirical findings of Barnett and Morse (1963) is no longer justified. At the same time, it is prudent to remember that extrapolation of present trends may provide a poor prediction of future events.

This raises the following questions: If there is a rise in the cost of extracting or using nonrenewable resources, especially energy resources, will this exert a major drag on the economic growth of the economy? To what extent will this drag be compensated for by technological progress in the nonextractive sectors? In an early paper, Nordhaus and Tobin (1972) argue that natural resource scarcity will not be an increasingly severe drag on economic growth given standard neoclassical assumptions and taking into account resource substitutability and technical change. In a later paper, Nordhaus (1974) specifically addresses the magnitude of the drag that shortages of energy resources might exert on economic growth. His estimates provide grounds for some optimism.

In the absence of technological change in the rest of the economy, he estimated that the real price of energy may on average rise by about 2.2 percent per year for the next 50 years, then by 1.2 percent annually for another 100 years, before levelling off due to the predominant use of nuclear energy. These predictions are not based on the increasing use of "soft" energy sources such as solar energy. They imply that the real price of energy will rise to about 3 times the current levels in 50 years and to 8 times current levels in 150 years. But the backstop of nuclear technology should result in energy prices not rising beyond this level. According to Nordhaus (1974), the expected lives of our known energy resources are extremely long. These are as follows:

If we rely on fossil fuels only:	550 years
+ current nuclear technology:	8,000 years
+ breeder technology:	1 million years
+ fission technology:	80 million years

Even given only current technology, the implied minimum 8,000-year life-span is a long one.

To the extent that these estimates are heavily influenced by reserve-production ratios, however, they may be overoptimistic. They are subject to considerable uncertainty. In particular, the perfection of breeder technology and fission technology remains uncertain, and nuclear waste disposal problems remain. Still, they do provide grounds for optimism for some time to come.

ASSESSMENT

While the economic growth prognosis of the Club of Rome seems overly pessimistic, the degree of optimism expressed by Julian Simon (1977) and Barnett and Morse (1963) seems misplaced. In particular, there is no guarantee that technical progress will be as conveniently accommodating as assumed by most of the growth optimists. Furthermore, there can be little doubt that our global economic position with continuing economic growth is becoming more precarious, in two ways:

1. technological progress must continue to proceed at a sufficiently rapid rate (a sufficient exponential rate?), and there is no guarantee that it will do so; and
2. global pollution is likely to become an increasing threat to production.

As Lecomber (1979, p. 32) points out, one of the certain things about the degree of future natural resource scarcity and limits to economic growth is its inherent uncertainty, because the past gives little guide to future technical possibilities. He goes on to suggest (correctly, in my view) that economic expansion has served to increase the level of uncertainty about the sustainability of production and economic growth. Both the absolute and the cumulative impact of economic production and the pace of change are such that risks to the environment and to the possibility of maintaining production are increasing (cf. World Commission on Environment and Development, 1987).

Growth has enormously increased man's capacity to do irreparable harm to the environment. Such harm, the unintentional by-product of modern technology, is increasingly international or global in impact, thus contrasting sharply with the much more local pollution problems of the Middle Ages. [Lecomber, 1979, p. 32]

Furthermore, he warns that an increasing proportion of production has become dependent on chemical processes and that the wastes from these may seriously disturb the ecological balance.

Most pessimists about the prospects for continuing economic growth concentrate their attention on the scarcity of nonrenewable resources and their imminent exhaustion. But we have already noted that as far as energy resources are concerned, they are likely to last for at least several hundred years and are not likely to be a major drag on economic growth. While we should not be complacent about nonrenewable resource-depletion, there are grounds for greater concern about reductions in the stock of our renewable biological resources, especially the rapid disappearance of species due to the economic activity of man and human population increases (IUCN, 1980).

While the extinction of species is a process that occurs naturally with evolution and environmental change, the rate of extinction has increased alarmingly due to man's activities, and consequently biological diversity is rapidly being decreased. Thereby (as discussed in Chapter 6), existing production is placed at greater risk because of the smaller gene bank and the consequently reduced ability of man to counteract unfavorable ecological change, such as the occurrence of a new serious disease in a major food crop. Furthermore, options for future economic use are lost. New knowledge can mean that a species that now appears to have no commercial value becomes of great value in the future, for medical or other purposes.

It ought in addition be borne in mind that as nonrenewable resources are depleted, men will become more dependent on living renewable resources to sustain economic production. To the extent that the stock of these resources is irreversibly reduced through the man-induced extinction of species, we undermine our ability in the very long term to sustain economic production and the human species. Given the presence of renewable resources, production may not completely collapse once depletable resources are exhausted, or almost so. However, the smaller the remaining stock of species, the lower is likely to be the level of sustainable production from renewable resources. In this sense, the existence of a diversity of species helps to provide long-term economic security for mankind.

Some may take the view that as mere mortals we should not be concerned with such seemingly far-off events as future resource poverty. However, disregard for our biological resources can impoverish mankind even in the short run by undermining economic production and reducing human satisfaction. A society that ignores the value of its biological resources is likely to impoverish itself both in the short and in the long run and may even encounter economic disaster more quickly than one that depletes only its nonrenewable resources. This is not to say that the use of non-renewable resources should be disregarded. Indeed, we should carefully consider the consequences of their rapid depletion for the productivity of our biological resources. Will their rapid depletion for economic purposes seriously reduce our stock of biological resources? Would a slower rate of depletion help to extend the productivity of our biological resources much longer? For example, would less reliance in the short run on artificial fertilizers help to maintain agricultural production at high levels for considerably longer? It is worthwhile, at least, to ask such questions even if the answers to them remain uncertain.

Certainly the above discussion is consistent with Maitra's (1988b) suggestion that

The ultimate solution to the resource problem . . . depends on how we would change our present consumption and production pattern, i.e., our life style dictated by consumerism, and on future population policy. We should not forget that population is the ultimate economic resource and the ultimate aim of all economic activities. Its quantitative and qualitative improvements are the only way out of all resource limitations to today and tomorrow.

But different writers have vastly differing expectations about our ability to improve human population quantitatively and qualitatively so as to escape tightening resource constraints. So we are still left with a fundamental uncertainty problem.

Two other concerns expressed by Maitra (1988b) are worth noting in conclusion. First, the major part of technological progress occurring in relation to the exploitation and use of energy resources is taking place in developed economies. It tends to be capital-intensive, which may not be in the economic interest of less developed countries, for whom more labor-intensive technology would be appropriate. International dualism between developed and less developed countries may be reinforced by this *regional* pattern of technological progress. Second, the time pattern of technological progress may be more influenced by adaptive and possibly myopic behavior than by rational expectations. For example, before 1970, the apparent abundance of oil seems to have led to the relative neglect of coal research. Maitra (1988b) questions in the light of increased shortages of oil whether the induced pattern of technological change has been optimal. In any case, his observa-

tions support concerns that the pattern and progress of technological change may be far from optimal and may even be unreliable.
Few, if any, grounds exist for being complacently optimistic that
technological progress will extricate us without fail from the predicament that we may face due to continuing economic growth and
careless and profligate use of nonrenewable resources to satisfy
high levels of aggregate consumption.

6

Preservation of Species, Crop Varieties, and Genetic Diversity

That the number of species and variety of species are diminishing rapidly in the world and are likely to continue to do so with economic growth is well documented (World Commission on Environment and Development, 1987, Ch. 6). This appears to be so both for wild and for domesticated species and means that the world is coming to rely on an ever-narrowing genetic base for its biological production. This may make it increasingly difficult to maintain economic production from biological resources. Given the smaller gene pool, it is harder to counteract a weakness such as reduced disease resistance by varieties of plants, animals, and other species used for economic production. This will become increasingly so unless miraculous progress is made in genetic engineering. Even with considerable progress in the latter, increasing obstacles can be expected due to lack of genetic building blocks. However, not only is the maintenance of existing production at risk but the scope for developing new types of biological production and commodities based on living organisms is being reduced. This being so, there is a *materialistic* economic argument in favor of conservation, even given a man-centered approach.

But economists do recognize that species can have economic value for other than materialistic purposes. Provided individuals are willing to pay for the preservation of a species, it has economic value, even if it has no commercial value as such. Nevertheless, until the 1970s almost exclusive attention was given in the economics of conservation of living organisms contributing to material production.

Not all arguments in favor of conservation are based on economics or on an anthropocentric approach. Some would argue that man has a responsibility or a moral duty to preserve nature or other sentient beings, irrespective of his own self-interest. Such views have, for example, been expressed by Aldo Leopold (1966) and appear to be increasingly accepted (Passmore, 1974). To the extent that these views are accepted in the community and individuals are willing to pay, they should be taken into account in the standard approach of welfare economics using, for example, the Kaldor–Hicks criterion.

But what if the willingness of people to pay (or to accept payment) to preserve a species is less than the cost of doing so once account has been taken of all the aspects mentioned above, including whatever moral obligation individuals feel toward other species? Strictly speaking, there is no economic argument for preserving the species. Yet the matter should not necessarily rest there. We may wish to ask such questions as,

1. how well informed are individuals about the species?

2. are their preferences likely to change?

3. to what extent is their valuation affected by the distribution of income, and is it "reasonable" that it be affected in the way it is by this distribution?

All of these matters having been considered, the argument for the preservation of a species may still be weak from society's point of view. However, there may be a group strongly in favor of preserving a species and prepared to take political and direct action to foster this cause. All sources of social conflict about species preservation cannot be resolved by rational argument or debate. Nevertheless, such argument can help to resolve some conflicts and specify our alternatives more precisely, thereby making for some progress.

This chapter has as its main objective the critical consideration of criteria suggested by ecologists and by economists as bases for deciding whether or not to save a species or an array of species or varieties from extinction. It suggests that the safe standard approach to the conservation of species is more compatible with minimax regret than with minimax loss. It also emphasizes the importance of applying the criteria in a trade-off or constrained resource availability situation, which means that greater attention is focused on opportunities foregone. Lastly, some observations are made about the reduction in the available varieties of crops with the introduction of high-yielding varieties.

In considering criteria or priorities for preserving species, let us in turn examine: (1) the priorities suggested in the World Conservation Strategy (WCS) (IUCN, 1980); (2) cost–benefit analysis (CBA) as, for example, used by the Resources for the Future group (RFF); (3) the safe minimum standard (SMS) approach based on minimax loss, as for example suggested by Ciriacy–Wantrup (1968) and Bishop (1979); (4) the alternative of SMS based on minimax regret; (5) the implications of these criteria in a constrained resource-availability situation; and (6) the compromise criterion, involving a compromise between CBA and SMS, as suggested by Randall (1986).

PRIORITIES FOR SPECIES PRESERVATION IN THE WORLD CONSERVATION STRATEGY

One of the aims of the World Conservation Strategy is to prevent the extinction of species and to preserve as many varieties as possible of crop plants, forage plants, timber trees, livestock, animals for aquaculture, microbes, and other domesticated organisms and their wild relatives (IUCN, 1980, sec. 6.4). This is seen as being important for two reasons.

1. to promote diversity of species to maintain biological stability (and presumably stability of economic production dependent on biological resources);

2. to keep options open for future possible use of species or varieties by Man open. The future value of many species and varieties is imperfectly known and surely future uses will be found that are as yet unknown.

Table 6.1
Priorities Suggested in the WCS Document for Conserving Species

Size of loss	Imminence of loss		
	Rare	*Vulnerable*	*Endangered*
Family	4**	2***	1***
Genus	7*	5**	3***
Species	9*	8*	6**

Notes: 1–9 Suggested order of priority
    *** Top priority
    ** Intermediate priority
    * Lower priority

Because of this uncertainty and the likelihood that new uses of species will be discovered, it is rational to keep options open or to retain flexibility, even at a cost (Hart, 1942; Tisdell, 1968, 1970). This requires us to err in favor of conserving species (Arrow & Fisher, 1974).

However, the WCS recognizes that varieties and species will continue to be lost and suggests that priorities need to be drawn up to choose what species to preserve. WCS suggests that priority should be given to the species where the loss is *large* and *imminent*. The size of loss is assumed to be higher depending upon whether only a single species, a whole genus, or a whole family is at stake. The imminence of the loss is said to depend on whether the species is rare, vulnerable, or endangered. The suggested system of priorities is shown in Table 6.1.

In this system of priorities, no specific account is taken of the benefits and costs of the preservation of a species, but the net benefit is assumed to be greater the more unique the species in relation to the biological classification system and the more imminent the loss (cf. Tisdell, 1983a). On the other hand, can we always assume that the benefit of saving a species that is the single representative of a whole plant or animal family is greater than that of saving a species that is less unique biologically but of great economic value? Should the costs involved in the conservation strategy by ignored? Should more effort be given to conserving endangered species rather than rare ones? In the last respect, if the costs are high and probability low of saving endangered species in relation to rare ones, it might be wiser to place more emphasis on ensuring that rare species do not become endangered.

While the WCS recognizes the importance of the interdependence of species and points out that the removal of a species that forms part of the food chain may result in the loss of dependent species, allowance for this is not incorporated specifically in the priority schema as represented in Table 6.1. But as Randall (1986) argues, it is of fundamental importance to address the issue for it determines the scope of the debate. Randall (1986, p. 101) says:

The ultimate instrumentalist argument—that every life form must be preserved in order to ensure the survival of the things people do care about and ultimately, of humanity—tends to deny, or at least sharply restrict, the possibility of setting priorities. . . .

Randall suggests that if the survival of all species depends on the survival of every single one, and if the disappearance of some is inevitable, then priorities may have to be about *the sequence* of disappearance of species on the way to the ultimate extinction of all. However, the extreme interdependence proposition is not universally accepted and, indeed, may not be commonly accepted. Nevertheless, even without accepting the extreme proposition that the removal of any one species seals the fate of all, interdependence between species is an important factor to take into account in determining whether or not a species should be saved from extinction.

While WCS does point out the case for conservation on the basis of uncertainty and keeping options open, this is not explicitly introduced into the WCS priority schema. Uncertainty about benefits provides a major rationale for approaches adopted by some economists to determining priorities for conserving species. Let us, therefore, consider their approach to this subject.

COST-BENEFIT, NET PRESENT VALUE APPROACH

The approach most widely used by economists in evaluating projects is cost–benefit analysis (CBA) based on calculations of net present values. This involves expressing as many benefits and costs in monetary terms as possible and quantifying wherever this can be achieved. The plan that maximizes the net present value of the resources used in its implementation is adopted.

Resources for the Future (RFF) has been very active in applying this approach, as reviewed by Chisholm (1988), to decisions about the preservation of species. RFF has extended "conventional criteria for optimal investment to take account of the irreversibilities associated with actions involving natural environments" (Smith & Krutilla, 1979). Nevertheless, a considerable amount of information or knowledge is assumed to exist about the payoffs from preserving species. When using CBA attempts are normally made to characterize uncertainty by probability distributions and to use expected gain or utility characteristics as a deciding factor. However, it is debatable whether such precision is possible or desirable.

It is frequently uneconomic to specify a decision problem precisely because the collection, organizing, and processing of data involves a cost. Bounded rationality may be optimal (Simon, 1957). Furthermore, no matter how many resources are allocated to data collection, it may be impossible to obtain reasonable approximations to benefits from conserving a species. In this regard Randall (1986, p. 95) says:

preservation of species problems are among those for which impediments to high-quality BCA are greatest. The procedure for BCA, once the various alternative strategies have been defined, involves identifying the physical consequences of each strategy, evaluating the physical consequences economically (i.e. costs and benefits), and calculating the net present value of each strategy.

Other writers, such as Ciriacy-Wantrup (1968) and Bishop (1978), argue strongly that the degree of social and natural uncertainty about the future possible value of a species is so great that it is unwise to try to apply CBA to decisionmaking in this area, and they suggest an alternative approach based on game theory.

SAFE MINIMUM STANDARD APPROACH— MINIMAX LOSS

As Ciriacy-Wantrup (1968) and Bishop (1978) believe that CBA is likely to be largely irrelevant to decisions about species preservation because of the degree of uncertainty involved, they suggest a safety-first approach that favors the preservation of a species at a safe minimum standard (SMS), that is, its conservation under conditions just sufficient to ensure its survival. This may, for example, necessitate a minimum amount of habitat for the species and a minimum breeding population. Bishop (ibid.) suggests that in relation to species conservation, the strategy that minimizes the maximum possible loss should be adopted.

For expository purposes, two alternative strategies and two possible alternative states of nature can be considered. Let two alternative strategies be (1) permit the species to become extinct, E, or (2) preserve it at a safe minimum level, SMS. Assume that the two possible alternative states of nature are (1) s_1, the species will have no economic value in the future and (2) s_2, the species will have a very large economic value in the future.

The available strategies and alternative states of nature and associated payoffs can be represented by the game matrix shown in Table 6.2. This matrix is similar to that used by Bishop (ibid.) to illustrate the SMS approach. In it, Y represents the maximum possible benefit from preserving the species (expressed as the loss from not conserving it), and C indicates the cost of conserving it. If the cost of saving the species is less than the maximum possible benefit of doing so, if $C < Y$, the minimax strategy is to adopt SMS, that is, to save the species from extinction by ensuring a safe minimum standard of conservation.

Table 6.2
Bishop-type Matrix

	s_1	s_2	Max loss
E	0	Y	Y
SMS	C	$C - Y$	C

Bishop (1978) and Ciriacy-Wantrup (1968) argue that as the cost of conserving a species is usually low and the possible or potential future benefits are extremely high, the optimal minimax loss strategy will almost always be SMS, to conserve the species at a safe minimum standard. One should, therefore, proceed on the presumption that conservation of a species is socially optimal until this is proven otherwise. This shifts the burden of proof to the anticonservationists. This point has been commented on by Randall (1986), and it will be taken up in subsequent discussion.

Although I am sympathetic to the general view of Bishop (1978) about nature conservation, some reservations are in order about the manner in which he presents the SMS approach using game theory. The problem is presented as a zero-sum game against nature. This assumes that nature is a rational maximizing opponent and that humanity's loss is nature's gain. But neither of these assumptions appears to be reasonable.

Nature does not have a "mind" and is not a rational opponent. Secondly, humanity's loss is often not nature's gain, and vice versa. In particular, if a species becomes extinct, humans may lose a benefit of Y, but does nature gain this amount? Presumably not. To the extent that the paradigm makes sense, nature, too, would seem to lose by extinction of a species.

SAFE MINIMUM STANDARD APPROACH— MINIMAX REGRET

This is not to say that minimax loss cannot be used as an extremely risk-averse strategy, even if the fundamental conditions of a zero-sum game are unsatisfied. However, it might be argued that if opportunity costs are important, a minimax regret rather than a minimax loss strategy would be more appropriate. For the problem as modeled by Bishop (1978), the minimax regret strategy turns out to be the same as that for minimax loss.

To see this, form the gain matrix for man shown in Table 6.3. This is the same as that for Table 6.2, except the values are multiplied by −1. From Table 6.3, the regret matrix shown in Table 6.4 can be formed.

From Table 6.4, it can be seen that SMS minimizes the maximum of regret, that is, the minimax strategy, if $C < Y$. Both minimax loss

Table 6.3
Man's Gain from Survival of Species

	s_1	s_2	Min gain if Y > C
E	0	$-Y$	$-Y$
SMS	$-C$	$Y - C$	$-C$

(or maximin gain) and minimax regret point toward the same policy conclusion in this case—namely, that since the costs of conserving a species are likely to be relatively low and the potential benefits high, conservation is to be favored.

Randall (1986) contends that from a political viewpoint the SMS approach involves a greater proconservation stance than CBA. In practice this is so, and proponents of SMS suggest that conservation of a species should be accepted as optimal until it is shown to be otherwise. SMS proponents suggest that in practice the costs of conservation of a species can be expected to be small in relation to potential gains. By contrast, cost–benefit analysts tend to suppose that a conservation project is not worthwhile until the benefits are shown to exceed the costs of the project. In the first case the *burden of proof* is placed upon those opposing conservation, whereas in the latter case it falls on those wishing to see a species conserved.

SMS as expounded does make it *more probable* than in the case of CBA that conservation will be favored. But even in the case of CBA it can be argued that the onus of proof should be on the opponents of conservation, given the presence of irreversibility, that is, given that the loss of a species is irreversible.

Table 6.4
Regret Matrix Corresponding to Table 6.3

	s_1	s_2	Max regret
E	0	Y	Y
SMS	C	0	C

CHOOSING WHICH SPECIES TO SAVE
GIVEN AN OUTLAY- OR RESOURCE-CONSTRAINT

In a world in which available resources or outlays for saving species from extinction are limited, a critical question is how the various criteria compare in selecting species for survival. In a situation of no such constraint, it is of course true that even in the absence of differences in direction of burden of proof, SMS will tend to lead to more species being saved than CBA and tends to support greater resource use for conservation. But what if the amount of resources for conservation is limited? Is the SMS approach equally desirable? Consider the various criteria in this context.

Suppose that K is the maximum outlay available for preserving all species. Where C_i is the cost of ensuring survival of the i-th species, choice is constrained by the requirement that $\sum C_i < K$. The various criteria discussed so far would result in the following choices:

1. CBA would select the array of species that would maximize net present expected value, that is, K would be allocated to saving species so as to maximize its present expected discounted value. Thus, species that have the highest expected discounted benefit in relation to costs when this criterion is applied will be favored for preservation.

2. The Bishop minimax loss or maximin gain approach results in preference being given to species with the highest *possible* benefit-to-cost ratios, that is, to those for which Y_i/C_i is highest. To do so, is to minimize the maximum possible loss per unit of outlay.

3. In order to minimize maximum possible regret, those species should be selected for which $(Y_i - C_i)/C_i$ is greatest. This will minimize maximum possible regret per unit of outlay. Note that because $(Y_i - C_i)/C_i = Y_i/C_i - 1$, this ordering will be the same as for the Bishop minimax loss ordering.

In the constrained situation both the minimax regret and the minimax loss criteria select the same species for preservation and are heavily influenced by the *maximum* possible or potential benefit from the species, whereas CBA selection is mainly determined by expected benefits that involve a weighting of possibilities.

However, Randall (1986) interprets the SMS approach differently to me in this context. He claims that SMS involves maximizing the number of species saved subject to the outlay constraint. He says, for example, in relation to his own criterion:

SMS logic would play the dominant role in establishing priorities. All species would be treated as having a positive but unknown expected value; implicitly all would be treated as equally valuable. Priorities would be set on the basis of opportunity costs; preserve that package which includes the most species given the cost constraint. [Randall, 1986, p. 103]

This assumes that uncertainty is so great that an estimate of the maximum possible value of species cannot be made and relies on the principle of insufficient reason in assuming that all species may be equally valuable.

Randall (ibid.) suggests a two-tiered approach to selecting species for preservation: (1) use CBA to the extent possible to make an initial selection; (2) for those species not selected because information is inadequate to apply CBA (or because of failure to meet the CBA test?), apply (his) SMS approach—that is, maximize the number of species saved in this group.

However, information is not nearly as dichotomous as Randall's approach assumes. Cases may not neatly fall into two sets, one in which information is sufficient to apply traditional CBA and another where ignorance is so great that no discrimination is possible between the maximum possible value of species. Degrees of uncertainty about the value of different species are likely to vary along a spectrum.

While CBA has its limitations in this area, neither of the SMS approaches as interpreted by me above are without difficulty, because species are ranked only by reference to extreme values. The following illustrates the problem: suppose that the smallest possible value of a species is not zero, but a value, V_i, which may be greater than zero. In addition, $V_i - C_i$ may be positive. So, even given the worst possible state of nature, there is a net benefit in saving the species. However the SMS strategy is influenced only by Y_i/C_i and not at all by V_i/C_i. Thus if Y/C is the same for two species, the SMS approach will rank them equally even though V/C may be very much higher for one of the species.

Where V represents the benefit from a species under the worst possible conditions and Y is its additional maximum potential value, Table 6.3 is modified in the way shown in Table 6.5.

It might also be observed that if the conservative view of "a bird in the hand being worth two in the bush" is adopted, a case might be made out for ranking species on the basis of V_i/C_i values, or at least a

Table 6.5
Man's Gain from Survival of a Species (Given that Its Minimum Value is V)

$$
\begin{array}{c}
\quad s_1 \qquad\quad s_2 \\
\begin{array}{cc}
\text{E} \\
\text{SMS}
\end{array}
\left[
\begin{array}{cc}
-V & -(V + Y) \\
V - C & V + Y - C
\end{array}
\right]
\end{array}
$$

weighting of these and Y_i/C_i values. But of course such a criterion as well as several others for choice under uncertainty, as for example reviewed by Chisholm (1988), have blemishes (cf. Tisdell, 1968). Furthermore, the degree and nature of knowledge about different projects or species can vary considerably, so one has to deal with a mixed system involving for some species certainty, in other cases probability, and in still other cases pure uncertainty, and yet make an "efficient" decision in relation to this *whole* collection. This problem has not been satisfactorily solved, even though Randall (1986) does at least implicitly deal with such a problem in his approach.

DISAPPEARANCE OF CROP VARIETIES
AND STABILITY OF PRODUCTION

Not only are wild species rapidly disappearing, but the number of varieties of domestic crops appears to be declining, and this is of concern to ecologists (Plucknett, Smith, Williams, & Anishetty, 1986). In developed countries, almost all the total production from major crops is typically supplied by three or four varieties of the crop, and primitive cultivars have largely disappeared (IUCN, 1980). As a country becomes more developed and high-yielding or improved varieties are introduced, traditional cultivars tend to disappear, and the genetic reserves available to scientists for breeding purposes decline.

Indications are that this happened in Greece (ibid.) and appears to be happening in Bangladesh (Tisdell & Alauddin, 1988) with the introduction of high-yielding varieties of rice. It is possible, especially where technology is introduced from abroad, for a number of varieties to increase at the same time as the fundamental gene bank for a species or a crop declines, that is, some genetic characteristics may be lost as a result of the loss of primitive cultivars, and new varieties may involve a smaller bundle of characteristics. So there is a difficult problem in measuring the extent of genetic diversity by a simple index.

This raises the question of whether there is market failure in the preservation of possible breeding traits or characteristics for animals and crops. While a case exists for applying economic criteria to breeding and crop improvement (McArthur, 1987), the economic system may fail to preserve sufficient genetic diversity in relation to animals and crops as a result of such factors as externalities, private attitudes to risks, and transaction costs (cf. Tisdell, 1982). Thus a case might be made for government intervention.

Scientists have suggested that reduced diversity of agricultural production and of varieties and species involved in this production will increase instability of production. While high-yielding varieties appear to be less tolerant to environmental stress than are traditional varieties (cf. Tisdell, 1983c) and reductions in mixed cropping seem to have occurred with economic development, there seems to have been also a reduction in the relative instability of crop production. Alauddin and Tisdell (1988a, 1988d) have shown that the relative instability of annual rice yields in Bangladesh has fallen with the introduction of high-yielding varieties. They attribute this to the increase in the incidence of multiple cropping and to greater control of the growing environment made possible by modern techniques and inputs. Evidence from elsewhere is also pointing toward a similar result (Hazell, 1986).

Nevertheless, despite an apparent reduction in the relative instability of yields with the introduction of high-yielding varieties, the long-term *sustainability* of agricultural production and yields may increasingly be at risk. Past data on variability of production and yields may fail to alert us to a rising danger in this regard (cf. Alauddin & Tisdell, 1988b).

CONCLUDING COMMENTS

Humanity's responsibility in relation to nature is a heavy one since we are increasingly in a position to determine which species will survive, and in any case our activities are expected to lead to the further disappearance of species. This responsibility cannot be avoided. However, we are in a weak position to decide rationally what species and varieties of living things to save from extinction and which to permit to become extinct. While advances, in part due to the effort of economists, have been made in understanding the issues involved in conservation of species and in seeing the complexity and economic importance of the problem, we are still a considerable way from resolving the issues, particularly given the degree of uncertainty inherent in evaluations. Nevertheless, the drift of economic thought over the last two decades or so has been increasingly in favor of conserving species, not only in the case of approaches based on the safe minimum standard, but also of those relying on cost–benefit analysis. Thus the view is increasingly gaining support that conservation of species should be the general rule, unless opponents can prove in a particular case that there is a net advantage in developments at the expense of species conservation. By altering the parties primarily responsible for the burden of proof in the conservation versus development debate, the chances of conserving species and coming closer to an optimal social solution may be improved. Those upon whom the burden of proof is placed have the greatest economic cost or risk in proposing a change or defending the status quo, as the case may be. The burden of proof also tends to define policies that will be permitted *unless* they are proved to be suboptimal. Thus the nature of the burden of proof is politically very important in the conservation debate.

7

Case Study in the Economics of Biological Conservation: Yellow-eyed Penguins and Wildlife on the Otago Peninsula

The Otago Peninsula, South Island, New Zealand, which extends from Dunedin, approximately 20 kilometers into the South Pacific Ocean, is a relatively unique natural resource, not only because of its geographical nature but because of the wildlife that it attracts and can support. Being situated in close proximity to Dunedin and because access to the area is relatively easy, it has considerable economic potential as a major tourist attraction, some of which is already being realized. However, for its full potential to be achieved, economic development and conservation in the area need to go hand in hand. It is increasingly being accepted that economic development, especially for tourist purposes, should be sustainable, and sustainability often requires that biological resources be conserved (Barbier, 1987; Conway, 1987; Tisdell, 1988b). Indeed, the World Conservation Strategy (WCS) (IUCN, 1980) argues that biological conservation is essential for sustainable development and that the objectives of conservation and development when truly considered are not in conflict. The WCS document also emphasizes that it is sometimes possible to make considerable economic gain by conserving wildlife and other biological resources as a drawcard for tourism.

At least in 1988, the full economic potential of the resources of the Otago Peninsula for tourism were not being realized.

First, there is no Interpretation Centre, providing an overview of the whole Peninsula—its geography, history, wildlife, etc.—as is, for example, the case in relation to Fiordland National Park, New Zealand. Second, its potential for outdoor recreation in terms of cycling, hiking, and so on by tourists may not be fully developed. Third, a number of wildlife species are underutilized for tourism purposes, and/or their survival is threatened so there is a danger of their disappearance from the Peninsula and the permanent loss of a tourist asset. The uniqueness of some of the wildlife on the Peninsula, such as the yellow-eyed penguin, and of the natural attractions of the Peninsula, is not well known to visitors to New Zealand. They need to be more widely advertised to encourage the average visitor to include a stopover in Dunedin in his/her New Zealand visit.

Wildlife conservation on the Otago Peninsula needs to be seen as an asset which, if more completely developed and promoted, can induce tourists to include a Dunedin stopover in their tour and tour operators and tourist agents to recommend it. To recommend such a stopover, the agent or operator needs to be convinced that the extra benefit to clients will exceed their extra cost or, if clients are on a limited time-budget, that the stopover represents considerable benefit to the client in relation to the time involved. In any case, wildlife conservation on the Otago Peninsula should be seen as a part of a plan to attract more tourists to Dunedin and to increase the length of stay of tourists in Dunedin. To the extent that this is successful, it will help increase incomes and employment in Dunedin.

In relation to the Otago Peninsula, it is useful to consider two species in particular, the royal albatross and the yellow-eyed penguin, from an economic viewpoint and in relation to the tourist industry.

THE ROYAL ALBATROSS COLONY:
TOURISM AND ECONOMICS

On the Otago Peninsula, the royal albatross *Diomedea epomophora* is the most intensively utilized wildlife species for tourism purposes, and it is useful to consider it as an indicator of the potential of wildlife as a tourist attraction. From a business enter-

prise point of view, the Royal Albatross Colony at Taiaroa Head
has a number of advantages. These are:

1. The amount of land that has had to be set aside for conservation is
relatively small. The opportunity cost of keeping the colony is small.

2. Exclusion from the site is relatively easy, so the service of conserving
species on the site for viewing can be sold to the public via entry fees. The
service can be marketed, as is done with most private goods. Nevertheless,
some individuals may see flying albatross from boats or from outside the
enclosure without paying.

3. Since the Otago Peninsula Trust, as authorized by the Department of
Conservation, has a monopoly (is the only operator able to sell rights to see
royal albatross colonies in the area), it can charge a monopoly price for
entry.

4. Because a high proportion of young albatrosses born in the colony
return to the colony to breed on reaching adulthood, there is a close
connection between attempts to conserve young in the colony and future
populations of royal albatross at the colony.

5. The site is easily accessible in virtually all weather conditions.

6. Not only albatross but also breeding colonies of shags can be seen as a
rule, and there is a magnificent view across the harbor, including Ara-
moana spit. So there is varied interest.

In short, the characteristics associated with the preservation of
the royal albatross are such as to make it a possible business
proposition.

This is not to say that the Otago Peninsula Trust is able to capture
all the economic benefits from the Royal Albatross Colony, but to
suggest that where the abovementioned characteristics are not
satisfied, it is more difficult for any body undertaking conservation
measures to appropriate economic gains from these. Furthermore,
it is likely that the Royal Albatross Colony is not run along strict
business enterprise lines with profit maximization or loss minimiza-
tion uppermost in the minds of its administrators.

The economic value of the Royal Albatross Colony to Dunedin
does not depend solely on the profit or loss on the enterprise. Given
that opportunities for earning income and obtaining employment in
Dunedin are limited, the colony makes a useful contribution to the
local economy by adding to local income and employment. This
contribution is much greater than might appear to be the case at first
sight.

Given 14,000 visitors per year (approximately the number in 1987) and an entry fee of NZ$8.00 per person (the 1988 fee), NZ$112,000 per year is earned by the colony from visitors' fees. With additional income earned from sales of souvenirs and similar items at the colony, gross income is likely to exceed NZ$112,000 per year. All of this income is spent, and it gives employment among other things to some 30 part-time guides.

Since most of the visitors to the colony (possibly 90%) are from outside Dunedin, most of the expenditure at the colony is a net addition to income in the local area. In round terms, this amounts to about NZ$100,000 per year, most of it spent locally on goods and services. If 66 percent of the income when respent goes on goods and services produced locally and 33 percent goes on goods and services brought in from other areas, the original injection of NZ$100,000 will create an addition to income in the Dunedin area of NZ$300,000 per year.

However, the story does not end there. Visitors who may have been induced to visit Dunedin because of the albatross colony or to stay an extra period of time in Dunedin will spend additionally, say, an extra NZ$50 on transport to the Colony, accommodation, etc. If there are 12,600 visitors from outside the region, this injects an additional NZ$630,000 into the local economy. But as it is respent, there is a multiplier effect on the local economy. Given a leakage of expenditure of 33 percent, an additional total contribution of NZ$1,890,000 results, which when added to the sum mentioned earlier means a *rise in local demand and income of almost NZ$2.2million per year*. This means the creation, for example, of 110 local jobs, at an average income of NZ$20,000 per year resulting from the colony. Even if the leakage from the local economy is somewhat higher than 33 percent per round of expenditure, clearly the colony results in considerable income and employment generation locally when direct and indirect effects are taken into account.

THE YELLOW-EYED PENGUIN:
ITS TOURIST ECONOMIC POTENTIAL

Compared to the royal albatross, the tourist potential of the yellow-eyed penguin *Megadyptes antipodes* is substantially under-developed, partly because the ecological nature of the species requires larger areas to be set aside for its breeding colonies, and suitable areas remain in the hands of several private property owners. This means that, unlike in the case of the royal albatross, there is no monopoly on the supply of viewing areas for yellow-eyed penguin (YEP) on the Peninsula. In the absence of government resumption of foreshore areas and the establishment of protected nature reserves, this position is unlikely to change. Unless all landholders willing to allow viewing access cooperate, the fee for viewing the YEPs is likely to be kept low by competition. Present landholders, therefore, have little incentive to develop the YEP as a tourist resource and may feel that other landholders would benefit from any initiative on their individual part.

There is a case for a nonprofit body such as the Yellow-eyed Penguin Trust, say, in cooperation with the Department of Conservation acquiring or obtaining control over a suitable viewing site or coming to a cooperative arrangement with a landholder to manage an existing site. This would provide a secure base for informing tourists and the public of the nature of the yellow-eyed penguin and of the conservation program, and a nucleus for selling related material and raising funds. As with the albatross colony, the ideal site might have additional attractions to yellow-eyed penguins.

In any case, it seems important that tourists be informed about the special nature of the YEP if the latter is to be fully appreciated. Fascination is partly a function of knowledge, as are our ideas of what is worth while. It is also important to have an easily accessible site available for viewing YEPs, whether this is operated privately, or by a public group, or by private/public cooperation. This is, of course, consistent with the major portion of protected areas not being available to the public.

As of April 1988, the privately operated viewing site "Penguin Place" charged NZ$3 per visitor, but no interpretative material was provided. This price is considerably lower than the fee for a visit to the Royal Albatross Colony. Presumably a higher price could be obtained if the attraction were more heavily promoted and developed with interpretative facilities and, in addition, if a larger number of visitors could be expected. Although there are other sites where one can see YEPs, these do not appear to be as accessible, nor are they publicized. No doubt a higher fee, perhaps NZ$6, could be charged if greater service were provided.

Table 7.1
Income Generated by Extra Tourists Attracted by Conserved and Promoted YEPs:* Some Alternative Possibilities (in NZ$m per year)

Extra number of tourists attracted or staying longer	Extra expenditure per tourist on local goods and services	
	$50	*$100*
1,000	0.15	0.3
5,000	0.75	1.5
10,000	1.5	3

*Assuming an income multiplier of 3.

The economic gains arising from tourism from saving the YEP on the Otago Peninsula are difficult to estimate. But its disappearance would mean a loss, that is much greater than fees collected for visits, say, to "Penguin Place"; a biological resource will have been lost that could have been used more intensively to promote tourism to the local area. If the YEP disappears from the Otago Peninsula, an economic *option* for the future will have been lost. It will be difficult, extremely costly, or impossible to reintroduce the YEP once it has disappeared from the Peninsula.

To obtain economic benefits from protecting YEPs in the local area it is not necessary to obtain a monopoly price from tourists wishing to view them. Provided YEPs attract additional visitors to Dunedin and/or existing visitors stay longer and spend extra on local goods and services, the local region obtains an economic benefit.

Some hypothetical possibilities are set out in Table 7.1, assuming the 66 percent of income received from tourists is respent locally so that there is a multiplier on local income and employment of 3. If, say, on account of YEP conservation there are 1,000 additional visitors to Dunedin and they spend on average an extra NZ$100 on local goods and services, NZ$0.3million per year in additional income is generated for the area. If 5,000 additional visitors can be expected, NZ$1.5million per year will be added to the local economy, assuming that each extra visitor on average spends $100. It can be seen that even on conservative estimates a substantial contribution could be made to the local economy.

To the extent that some local production of wool, mutton, and so on has to be foregone to secure protected areas for YEPs, this has to be offset against the gains from extra tourism. But this is likely to be small in comparison; it could be estimated by, for example, taking the number of sheep displaced from reserves and estimating the annual net income that would have been earned from them.

All considered, it is not unreasonable to expect an addition of at least NZ$1 million per year to local income as a result of a program that successfully promotes the YEP as a tourist attraction. Such promotion is one of the objectives the Yellow-eyed Penguin Trust has in mind.

OTHER SPECIFIC ECONOMIC ASPECTS OF SAVING THE YELLOW-EYED PENGUIN

The main reason for saving YEPs on the New Zealand mainland and on the Otago Peninsula need not be their economic benefits from a tourist point of view, even though this aspect cannot be ignored. It may, indeed, be that a number of individuals are willing to pay or to dedicate property for reserves for YEPs in the mere knowledge that this will help to save YEPs from extinction on the mainland. This may be the main objective of the Yellow-eyed Penguin Trust—namely, to ensure survival of the YEPs on the mainland.

But even in that respect economic factors cannot be ignored. The extent to which individuals are willing to donate to the YEP Trust and support its activities may depend on perceived economic benefits as well as their opportunities to view and to come into contact with YEPs. Some compromise in conservation strategies in relation to YEPs may be needed to cater for human interest and curiosity about YEPs.

One of the objectives the Yellow-eyed Penguin Trust may have in mind is maximizing the population of YEPs on the mainland relative to whatever resources are placed under its control. Techniques for managing protected areas need to be assessed in terms of their productivity in maintaining YEP populations or increasing them, given this objective. Darby (1987) has discussed the possible efficiency of different types of revegetation programs in terms of the likely number of nesting sites provided, assuming that nesting site availability and not, say, the availability of food, is the main long-run constraint to the population in an area. Darby (1987) opts in favor of plantings of New Zealand flax in circles and suggests an overall habitat rehabilitation and planting strategy for conserved areas which also takes into account ecological methods of deterring introduced predators of penguin chicks such as ferrets and feral cats, bearing in mind that the population of ferrets is heavily dependent on rabbit populations.

It may, however, be necessary to modify the plan in some instances, such as at a tourist site, so as to allow visibility for the tourist and/or create a more attractive setting for the tourist experience. I am not sure how effective an outside grassy buffer zone is likely to be in deterring rabbits from entering a protected area, and how difficult and costly it will be to maintain. However, some landowners may want a windbreak or shelter for their stock if they forego foreshore areas, and this may have to be accommodated in some way if they are to be induced to make a larger area of land available for the protection of the YEP.

It is difficult to determine the total area that will have to be placed under protective management to save YEPs on the Otago Peninsula, since clearly complex ecological factors have to be taken into account. Even 100 hectares, if well managed and located, could make a substantial difference, although for safety's sake a somewhat larger area may be needed.

Using Darby's (1987) data, 100 hectares could support between 100 and 350 breeding pairs of YEPs, depending on vegetation—say, an average of 150 to 200 breeding pairs. This is slightly greater than the estimated number of pairs on the Otago Peninsula in 1987, namely, 130 to 140 breeding pairs. To return to the estimated number of breeding pairs in 1985–86 (305+), approximately 200 hectares of well-managed reserve would need to be set aside. This is *not* an exceptionally large area to conserve a species that could add considerably to local tourism and which is of great interest in itself.

The proposed conservation measures may attract other species of penguin to the area and assist the little blue penguin in its breeding, thus making an added attraction for tourists.

Apart from the land cost (about NZ$150,000 for 150 hectares, given that the average price per hectare on the Peninsula is NZ$1,000) in the YEP conservation programme, there are other costs, such as for fencing and revegetation, which no doubt the Trust has calculated.

The Trust is dependent for its success on enough landholders making available sufficient land in YEP breeding areas for the Trust to carry out its management strategy. To the extent that existing landholders are willing to convenant land, lease it at a nominal rent or to sell it to the Trust below market value, this will assist the Trust to reach its objective with limited public funding. But even with such assistance, the fund will need considerable financial support from the public to implement its management plan.

The Trust has indicated that it plans to launch a major fund-raising campaign. It says:

The object of fund raising is to enable breeding areas to be fenced and revegetated. It is hoped that landowners will covenant or lease suitable land. If land owners wish to sell, the Trust will purchase land and arrange reserve status. The Trust also plans to raise public awareness of the species, which is a popular focus for tourist activities in the region. [Yellow-eyed Penguin Trust, 1988]

Incidentally, like the royal albatross, there is a close connection between conservation of yellow-eyed penguins at a site and return of their young to the site. It seems that approximately 50 percent of surviving young return to the area where they were born (Yellow-eyed Penguin Trust, 1987, p. 3). So there will be a close relationship between YEP conservation effort on the Otago Peninsula and the permanent population of YEPs there.

OVERALL DESIRABILITY (ECONOMIC AND OTHERWISE) OF SAVING THE YELLOW-EYED PENGUIN

Little blue penguins and YEPs nest on the Otago Peninsula. It is worth while comparing the tourist value of the little penguin with the potential of that for the YEP. In Australia, the little or fairy penguin *Eudyptula minor* is the basis of a multimillion-dollar tourist industry on Phillip Island in Victoria. In 1985/86, 350,000 people visited Phillip Island to see these penguins, and the number of visitors is growing at 12 percent per annum. This species is also present in New Zealand. The variety that occurs in the Otago, Southland, and west coast areas of the South Island of New Zealand is the southern blue penguin. Yet the little penguin seems less suitable as a tourist attraction than the yellow-eyed penguin. It generally comes ashore after sunset and returns to the sea before sunrise, presumably to avoid land predators. The yellow-eyed penguin, on the other hand, arrives before sunset when it is possible to take photographs without a flash. No artificial lighting is required to view it, as in the case of the fairy penguin. Furthermore, little penguins usually nest in burrows and spend the night in these, which once again reduces their visibility, whereas the yellow-eyed penguin nests on the ground. YEPs can be seen all the year round on the Otago Peninsula.

The yellow-eyed penguin is taller than the little penguin and about five times as heavy, which makes it a rather more substantial visible subject for tourists. Stahel and Gales (1987, p. 16) report that the yellow-eyed penguin has an average body length of 60 cm and a weight of 5.2 kg, whereas the little penguin has a height of 40 cm and a body weight of 1.1 kg.

In terms of uniqueness, the yellow-eyed penguin has a strong claim for a high priority for conservation. It is the *only species of its genus*. Of the six genera of living penguins, its genus and that of the little penguin are the only ones with a single species. Its breeding population has been much reduced, and the long-term survival of the species may well be at risk. There is a danger that its breeding populations will be eliminated from the New Zealand mainland (Otago and Southland). It would then have breeding colonies only in Stewart Island, Codfish Island, Chatham Island, and Auckland Island, and these may become less viable due to greater inbreeding.

The yellow-eyed penguin is unique in that it is not a colonial species. It is believed by many scientists to be the most ancient living species of penguin. Species pair off and as adults remain in the vicinity of their nesting grounds throughout the year. They prefer to nest in timbered coastline habitats, and the disappearance of wooded or suitably vegetated coastline areas has been a factor in reducing the population of YEPs (Darby, 1987).

It is worth noting that this species (and genus) of penguin is unique to New Zealand. Only three distinct species of penguin have the New Zealand mainland as their normal range, according to Stahel and Gales (1987). Apart from the yellow-eyed penguin, the Fiordland penguin *Eudyptes pachyrhynchus* is the other unique species there, and there are five different living species in the genus *Eudyptes*. In addition, the Snares Island penguin, which is unique to the New Zealand ornithological region, can be seen occasionally on the Otago Peninsula, and the Fiordland crested penguin, the erect-crested penguin, the royal penguin, and the rockhopper penguin sometimes visit the Otago Peninsula (Yellow-eyed Penguin Trust, 1987).

On the basis of degree of uniqueness and imminence of loss, it is clear that the yellow-eyed penguin qualifies for a high priority for conservation under the guidelines set out in the *World Conservation Strategy* (IUCN, 1980; also see previous chapter of this book). It is the only species of its genus, and it must at least be regarded as vulnerable, which would give it the same priority as an endangered species using the World Conservation Strategy document's rating. If it is actually considered to be endangered (as may not be unreasonable), it would be rated as having a top priority for conservation. In any case, the method of setting priorities for conserving species as set out in the World Conservation Strategy document indicates that *this species should be given a high priority for conservation*.

Tentative cost–benefit analysis also suggests a high benefit–cost ratio from conserving the YEP, at least on the Otago Peninsula. It was suggested in a previous section that the land cost of saving the YEP on the Otago Peninsula would be about NZ$150,000. Additional capital costs are unlikely to exceed NZ$50,000. If the land value represents the present discounted value of the land in other uses, then about NZ$200,000 would represent the value of resources foregone from alternative uses to save the YEP on the Otago Peninsula. With the real rate of interest at 5 percent and the preservation of YEPs there providing a net benefit of NZ$10,000 per annum or more in perpetuity, then the project is economic on cost–benefit grounds; if a real rate of interest of 10 percent is applied, an annual net benefit of NZ$20,000 per year or more would be required to make the project economic. If the residents of Dunedin are prepared to pay 10 to 20 cents per year to retain YEPs on the Otago Peninsula, this would be sufficient to justify the project. Considering that the YEP project could add NZ$1 million per year in demand for goods and services in the Dunedin area, this would be a small amount. The people of Dunedin may, however, be prepared to fund the project on other grounds: they may value the existence of YEPs in their area independently of the ability of the YEPs to attract tourists.

The existing yellow-eyed penguins may be valued beyond Dunedin. If residents of the South Island were on average prepared to pay 1 to 2 cents per year to ensure the continued existence of YEPs on the Otago Peninsula, the project would be justified on social benefit–cost grounds, even neglecting other benefits. For the whole of New Zealand, a willingness to pay an average of around a quarter of one cent per year would be enough to justify the project. But there are also individuals not resident in New Zealand who would value the preservation of this species on the Otago Peninsula. A priori, the social and economic benefits of conserving the yellow-eyed penguin on the Otago Peninsula appear certain to exceed costs and are likely to do so by a substantial amount.

This conservation project may also be justified on the safe minimum standard argument for conserving species (Ciriacy-Wantrup, 1968; Bishop, 1978). To the extent that preservation of a breeding population on the Otago Peninsula is important in ensuring the survival of this species and given that the cost of conserving a population on the Peninsula is relatively low, the safe minimum standard argument would favor their conservation. It is clear that the maximum *potential* benefit from preserving YEPs on the Otago Peninsula far exceeds the cost of doing so. Risk avoidance, especially from the point of view of minimizing maximum possible regret, favors a strategy for conserving the species.

The yellow-eyed penguin is claimed to be the world's rarest penguin (Yellow-eyed Penguin Trust, 1987, p. 4). In 1985–86, it was estimated to have a breeding population of about 1,800 breeding pairs; of these, about 600 were located on the New Zealand mainland, approximately half of them on the Otago Peninsula. Estimates for 1987 by Darby indicate a considerable decline in breeding numbers on the New Zealand mainland. The number of breeding pairs seems to have approximately halved (Yellow-eyed Penguin Trust, 1987). There is little doubt that this rare species is now regionally endangered.

FURTHER DISCUSSION OF TOURIST DEVELOPMENT

Other species on the Otago Peninsula that could also be made greater use of for tourism but are at present only used in a casual manner include (1) the New Zealand fur seal; (2) the Stewart Island shag (of which the breeding colony on the Peninsula is said to represent about half of the New Zealand population) and other species of shag; (3) other sea birds, including the introduced black swan; and (4) possibly species of penguin other than the YEP, such as the southern blue penguin. A seal and whale attraction might also be worthwhile; this might be considered in the neighborhood of the Royal Albatross Colony if such an attraction could be established without loss of visual amenity. Interesting historical material relating to these mammals is available, and at least New Zealand fur seals can be viewed in the area. In the long term, even whale watch cruises may be a possibility. These are, for example, a commercial proposition in parts of the United States, for example, in the Cape Cod area. In addition, there may be some tourist interest in the local commercial fisheries of the area, both in relation to operations inshore as well as further afield, for example, on the Chatham Rise. In this respect the squid is a particularly interesting species, yet the display at the University of Otago's Marine Research Station at Portobello does not cater for it. In the United States, at Woods Hole, Massachusetts, the U.S. government has built an aquarium/ museum along these lines which both informs and aims to promote the demand for fish, since the funding authority is the Department of Commerce.

While not all the above can be developed at once, and some, on further scrutiny, may prove to be uneconomic, a large number of tourism possibilities related to biological resources exist in the Dunedin area. (In this respect, even the feral goats and feral geese of the Taieri Gorge have some interest.) It may be desirable to draw up priorities for the development of the tourist potential of these resources. Clearly the YEP should be high on this list, given its current tenuous position on the Otago Peninsula and that it is already being used as a tourist attraction, albeit less effectively than seems possible.

While Dunedin has tended to promote itself as the "Edinburgh of the South," this is unlikely to be a major drawing point for tourists, especially as far as visitors from the Northern Hemisphere are concerned. Relatively unique natural features are likely to be a greater attraction.

One question that needs to be considered is whether tourist promotion of additional biological and natural resources in the Dunedin area will mean excessive extra competition between attractions for the tourist dollar. Is Dunedin trying to divide up a fixed tourist pie? In my view such developments may be more complementary than competitive. Economic gains can be made by all attractions if more tourists are enticed to visit the area or if tourists are induced to stay long enough. Dunedin has sufficient natural attractions which, if correctly developed, conserved, and promoted, can make it a more strongly sought-after tourist destination on the South Island. Some threshold of tourist development, promotion, and infrastructure may need to be reached before large gains occur in terms of extra tourist visits. Also it should be borne in mind that it is sometimes useful to have more attractions than can be seen or experienced on one visit, since this may help induce future visits, as well as leaving a little mystery. It should also be remembered that it takes time for tourist promotion to have an effect and that the recommendations of those who have already visited an area can have a significant impact in the long run. The proposed program of the Yellow-eyed Penguin Trust can be seen as part of a program of natural resource conservation, development, and promotion to attract more tourists to the south of the South Island of New Zealand and retain them longer. There is probably a case for developing a regional strategy in this regard.

CONCLUDING COMMENTS

This chapter has illustrated how wildlife can have considerable economic value for tourism as well as from other points of view. Conservation of the yellow-eyed penguin in particular raises many interesting and special issues in economic evaluation, including the question of how to allow for the existence value of such a rare species.

8

Biological Control of Pests and Sustainable Development

THE IMPORTANCE OF THE BIOLOGICAL
CONTROL OF PESTS

The economic value of the biological control of pests such as weeds and insects is often taken for granted, but such natural controls are important resource assets. Natural ecological relationships help keep pests and diseases under control, and their importance manifests itself when these relationships are disrupted. In the absence of natural checks and balances, we risk being swamped by them. Natural balances can be disrupted by environmental changes such as reduced biological diversity brought about as a side-effect of growing economic production, or they can arise as a result of the use of pesticides or other artificial technologies.

Some pesticides have proven not to be effective in the longer term because target species have developed resistance to them. Furthermore, it is not uncommon for insecticides to destroy useful insects as well as pests. Useful insects may predate on the target species and so their destruction may contribute to an increase in the population of the targeted pest. In addition, insects that had been exerting a control on other potential pests may be destroyed. Even though the population of the targeted pest may be reduced, another specie or species may become a serious pest as a result of the use of an insecticide.

For several reasons, users of pesticides may become locked into these once they have begun to use them, in a sort of pesticide addiction (van den Bosch & Messenger, 1973, p. 122), and short-term advantages can be outweighed by long-term disadvantages. Benefits for an individual of the use of an insecticide can be unsustainable, but the short-term costs of withdrawal may be high. Individual producers may also be locked into pesticide-use as the result of side-effects or externalities caused by the use of pesticides by others; for instance, if the population of mobile predatory insects of a pest has been reduced in an area or a general build-up in the population of a mobile pest has been caused, so raising the cost to the individual (in terms of profit foregone) of not using the insecticide. In practice these are serious problems. The adverse economic and ecological consequences that *may* arise from using pesticides are well documented (ibid.; DeBach, 1974)). Their occurrence can be traced in part to market failure and in part to information failure (Tisdell, Auld, & Menz, 1984).

There are cases where "technological fixes" have proved themselves to be unsustainable and even counterproductive in their productivity-enhancing effects. Both the economic and the ecological ramifications of the new pesticide technologies have at times been inadequately assessed. In this regard, van den Bosch and Messenger (1973, p. 119) observe:

. . . after 1945, when the powerful synthetic organic insecticides appeared, they made insect suppression so easy and effective that virtually every other method of pest control was dropped in favor of these miracle chemicals as our insect control "crutch." But in neglecting the investigation and development of alternative controls we rendered ourselves vulnerable to insect depredation in the event that the chemicals failed. Very few imagined that this would ever come about. But today it is happening. . . .

In addition, however, there are worrying irreversibilities involved when the use of chemicals alters the genetic nature of a species or the composition of natural populations or causes the disappearance of species. A well-known effect of the use of DDT, for example, is its increasing concentration as it moves along the food chain. Its use

increased the incidence of infertility in birds of prey as well as causing them to lay soft-shelled eggs, so threatening the continued existence of some species. To the extent that man values the continuing
existence of such species either for their direct economic role in the
productive process or because of sheer existence-value, such
adverse spillover effects are a matter for economic concern.

Interest in the use of biological methods of controlling pests has
grown with our concern about the possible environmental impact of
the use of chemicals. While the use of natural enemies of pests to
control pest populations appears to be relatively ancient (the
ancient Chinese used this method) the use of classical methods of
biological control of pests is recent. Classical methods involve the
introduction of an exotic natural enemy (enemies) of a pest, usually
from the country of origin of the pest, and they are generally most
effective against introduced pests rather than indigenous ones.
Modern interest in the classical biological control of pests dates
from the period 1888–1889, the time when the United States
Department of Agriculture sent Koebele to Australia to obtain a
parasite to control cottony cushion scale, which had seriously
reduced citrus production in California. He found that the vedalia
ladybird beetle attacked this scale, and he sent some of these
beetles to California. On his journey home via New Zealand, he
also collected a large number of vedalia beetles near Napier for
shipment to California (DeBach, 1974, p. 96). They proved to be a
very successful means of biological control (Huffaker &
Caltagirone, 1986) and created continuing interest in this method of
pest control.

Even the economic benefits of the classical biological control of
pests are vast and run into billions of dollars (Tisdell, 1988a, 1989).
For Australia alone, this economic value is likely to exceed A$1
billion. To take just two cases, the economic benefits of biological
control of skeleton weed is estimated to exceed A$261 million,
assuming a discount rate of 10 percent and given 1975 prices (Marsden et al., 1980), and the Industries Assistance Commission (1985)
estimated a benefit–cost ratio of more than 10:1 for the biological
control of weeds of the *Echium* species. The economic benefits to
Australia of having controlled prickly pear (some Opuntia spp.) by
biological means is enormous. The economic significance of the
issue can hardly be overemphasized.

Nevertheless, although natural scientists have given and continue to give considerable attention to the biological control of pests, economists have given little attention to its economics and to methods of estimating the economic benefits of such control. Headley (1985) attributes this to a lack of cooperation between natural scientists and economists. He suggests that natural scientists undertake experiments and collect data and only consult economists when they believe that they have economically promising results; however, the data collected are often not in a form that can be used by economists, and usually resources are unavailable at this stage to rework the data to make it of value for economic evaluation. He suggests that economists should be consulted at an earlier stage so that they can indicate the sort of scientific data that would be needed for economic evaluation. As Randall (1986) has observed, economists live high on the information chain and cannot easily compensate for defects in information obtained from lower links. Nevertheless, this does not completely excuse the relative neglect of this area by economists.

BIOLOGICAL CONTROL AS AN ECONOMIC GOOD

When discussing biological control of pests, most writers have classical biological control in mind. In the case of pure classical biological control, the biocontrol agent spreads and reproduces of its own accord. All who are affected by the pest benefit from the introduction of the biocontrol agent, irrespective of whether they have contributed to its introduction. The control is a pure public good in that the agent introducing the biocontrol can only appropriate a small fraction of its benefit (say by initial use on his own property or sales to others requiring rapid diffusion onto their property). The characteristics of nonappropriatability and nonexclusion are satisfied (Tisdell, Auld, & Menz, 1984).

As the group of beneficiaries may be large, they are unlikely to be able to cooperate to introduce or search for a biocontrol agent, and its introduction is unlikely to occur unless the cost of this is very low in relation to the benefit of one or a few individuals. Nevertheless, the usual type of economic failure associated with pure public goods can be expected to apply: they will be undersupplied or not supplied at all unless public intervention takes place. There is, therefore, a case for public intervention. This is not to say that the general public should pay for the whole cost of such intervention. A case can be made out for any group of farmers who are expected to benefit to contribute, through a compulsory levy, for example, so as to overcome the free-rider problem.

There are also other reasons why the government may wish to intervene. The target pest may not be regarded as a pest by all in society—some may regard it as an asset. This, for example, is the case in Australia for Paterson's curse, *Echium* species. Apiarists in South Australia see this weed as an asset, whereas wheat growers in the Eastern states of Australia consider it to be a pest. Similar conflict exists in relation to other weeds, such as the blackberry. In such circumstances, it is necessary to weigh up the net gains and net losses of different interest groups to determine whether a positive economic gain overall can be expected from the introduction of a biocontrol agent. One might also expect the public decision about whether to introduce or permit introduction of a biocontrol agent to be influenced by its consequences for the distribution of income.

But even if a living organism is regarded by everyone as a pest, public intervention may still be required in the introduction of biocontrol agents because there is a risk (in some cases) that the biocontrol agent will attack nontarget species, to the detriment of those valuing these. The likelihood of this needs to be assessed and social net benefits need to be estimated taking into account nontarget prospects before a biocontrol agent is introduced.

It is important to undertake the above-mentioned social evaluation in advance of the introduction of a biocontrol agent because in most cases its introduction is for all intents and purposes *irreversible*. There is always the risk that the losses imposed by the introduction of a biocontrol agent may be very high when it attacks nontarget species or adapts to the new environment in unexpected ways. Thus *risk* or uncertainty is an important consideration in the decision-making process. This tends to favor extended search or testing and delay before the introduction of a biocontrol agent, even when only expected gains are to be maximized. In this context, this is analogous to Arrow and Fisher's (1974) argument that irreversibility when combined with uncertainty of benefits from conserving a resource should lead us to err in favor of its conservation, even if it is intended to maximize expected gain (see also Tisdell, 1970).

However, not all biological pest control is of the pure classical type. Scientist usually mention (1) augmentative, and (2) inundative biological control as further possibilities. In addition, integrated pest management (IPM) may be discussed under biological control.

Augmentative biological control involves measures to augment or supplement the population of the control species either in some regions or over time or both. For instance, in some regions of Australia, cold winters in the southern reaches of the distribution of the "prickly pear" cactus reduce the population of the introduced cactoblastis insect. In such areas the Prickly Pear Destruction Board releases additional populations of cactoblastis insects in the Spring. Again in some parts of Australia, the mosquito is either absent or seasonally absent in some areas infested by rabbits. The mosquito is the normal vector of the introduced myxomatosis virus, but this is augmented in areas where mosquitos are absent or in low numbers by the periodic release of rabbit fleas, which also act as vectors. These are bred at the Commonwealth Serum Laboratories in Victoria. From an economic point of view, the externalities or public good benefits of regional augmentation are *usually* limited to the region concerned, and so if one adopts the principle that the one who benefits ought to pay, regional beneficiaries ought to pay.

Inundative biological control refers to the application of the biocontrol agent in large quantities. The benefits of this are frequently localized to the area of application or not far beyond this. In the limiting cases, externalities are absent, and the control is a pure private good. The biocontrol agent can, therefore, be marketed in the same way as any other private good. In fact, companies are doing just that and are searching for new biocontrol agents that are pure private goods. For example, a bacterium, *Bacillus thurigiensis*, is on sale for spraying on plants for the control of caterpillars. Mycoherbicides (herbicides based on fungi) have been developed and are being marketed in the United States for the control of weeds. Research in the area is developing rapidly.

Integrated pest management (IPM) is not always considered as a part of biological control, as it does not involve the physical introduction of biocontrol agents. Nevertheless it is relevant, since it takes into account ecological factors in devising a pest control strategy. This may, for example, involve the preservation of habitat that favors populations of natural predators of the pest or the use of cultural practices that result in an unfavorable habitat for the pest. Some externalities beyond the firm may be generated by IPM, but they are usually of limited geographical range. IPM is the method of pest control favored in *Our Common Future* (World Commission on Environment and Development, 1987, pp. 136–137), which recommends that pest control be increasingly based on natural methods.

It might also be noted that biological pest control is an area in which genetic engineering and modification has economic potential and is already being used. For example, more virulent forms of myxomatosis are being developed as rabbits become more resistant to existing strains in Australia. Many developments in this area can be seen as part of development of the biotechnology industry generally.

EVALUATION OF THE ECONOMIC BENEFITS OF BIOLOGICAL CONTROL

Let us now consider briefly the evaluation of the economic benefits of classical biological pest control in an economic static setting, concentrating on social evaluation using the Kaldor–Hicks criterion. But it should be noted in advance that the problems associated with evaluation depend upon the stage of the biocontrol project. In the early stages, for example, uncertainty is likely to be considerable, but as the project progresses and more information comes to hand, uncertainty is much reduced. As decision-making involves costs, as Simon (1961) and Baumol and Quandt (1964) have pointed out, bounded rationality may be optimal in relation to decision-making.

We shall assess some means (shortcuts and otherwise) that have been used to indicate the possible economic benefits of classical pest control and isolate circumstances under which they may be reasonably accurate indicators of social benefits assuming that costs and benefits are confined to a single industry. Many of these indicators have been used by natural scientists rather than economists.

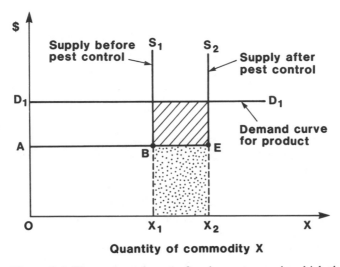

Figure 8.1 Illustration of *particular* circumstances in which the extent of reduction in the size of the pest population can be a useful indicator of the size of social benefits from biological pest control.

Extent of reduction in pest population: If the social economic loss from a pest population varies linearly with its size, then economic benefit arising from its control will be in proportion to the reduction in its population given classical control. Assuming that only one product is affected by the pest, the linear relationship will be satisfied if the quantity of production varies in a constant proportion to the population of the pest, unit costs of production are constant, and the demand curve is perfectly elastic, which implies that the price is not altered by a greater supply of the product. This is illustrated in Figure 8.1 for a commodity X. Prior to biological control, supply of the product is X_1, and the industry supply curve is ABS_1. After biological pest control, supply increases from X_1 to X_2, and the supply curve becomes AES_2. Given that the elastic demand curve D_1D_1 applies, social net gain can be measured by the hatched rectangle.

In the case shown in Figure 8.1, all the economic gains from biological pest control go to the producers of product X. But if the demand curve for the product is not perfectly elastic, some gains go to consumers through price reductions, and total social gains will be smaller than indicated by the hatched rectangle. If extra land is also brought into production as a result of the biological control and the costs of production on this land are not the same as on existing land, this may have to be allowed for. Still in some circumstances and at least over a range, the extent of the reduction in the size of the pest populations can be a useful indicator of the size of social benefits from biological pest control.

Increased yields and levels of production: The extent of increased yields or the rise in the quality of production can be used as a measure of the proportionate extent of social gains from biological control in some circumstances. This is possible in the case shown in Figure 8.1. In this case, however, one does not have to assume that yields or levels of production are linearly related to the level of the pest population, at least over a range.

Increased revenue: In the linear model, the *proportionate* increase in revenue is also an indicator of the proportionate rise in social benefit. But the *absolute* rise in revenue overstates the increase in social benefit, if price is constant and total costs rise on account of the greater production. In the case illustrated in Figure 8.1, the overstatement would amount to a quantity equal to the area of the dotted rectangle.

Increased aggregate net farm or enterprise profits: This is an accurate measure of social benefit if the price of the product does not fall as a result of increased production due to the biological control of a pest. But if the price of the product falls, this measure will understate the gain in social welfare, since it takes no account of the increase in consumers' surplus. In addition, it should be noted that in this analysis it is being assumed that the biological control has no external effects on other industries.

Cost savings due to the replacement of pesticides or nonbiological methods of control: This will tend to understate the social benefits unless stemming benefits are very small, as they will tend to be if demand for the product is relatively inelastic or the supply curve is relatively inelastic. It will understate social benefits in the normal case even assuming that biological control is just as effective as

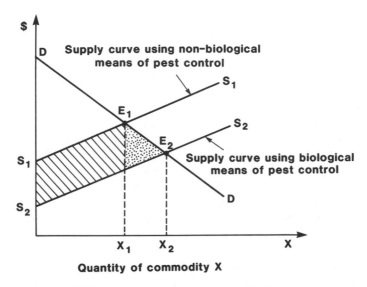

Figure 8.2 If biological control replaces nonbiological control of a pest, such as pesticide use, the cost saving from the elimination of nonbiological control methods will as a rule understate the net economic benefits of biological control.

nonbiological methods, because biological control, unlike nonbiological methods, does *not* as a rule involve marginal cost. This is illustrated in Figure 8.2. With nonbiological control of a pest, per unit cost of production in the industry falls, and the supply curve shifts from S_1S_1 to S_2S_2. Cost savings on existing production equivalent to the hatched area occur, but total benefits exceed this because a new equilibrium is established at E_2, and this results in stemming benefits indicated by the area of the dotted triangle.

Note that social gains from a new biological control should be measured relative to the use of existing pest control techniques. Absolute rather than comparative gains overstate the social value of a new control technique. I shall return to this point later.

Variations in land values: When a successful agricultural technique such as a biological pest control is introduced and raises the returns to be had from agricultural land in various locations, the market value of that land can be expected to rise, and the rent paid for its use may also rise. Under a number of circumstances, the total rise in the value of land due to the introduction of a biological control is an accurate indicator of the economic benefit from the control. The increased value of the land reflects the capitalized value of extra profits available from the land on account of the release of the biological control.

This is not to say that variations in land values necessarily capture all economic benefits. They may be influenced by speculation or by other developments, in addition to the introduction of the biological control, and some benefits may be obtained by consumers of agricultural products rather than producers, for example, through lower prices for products, and this will not affect land values.

Aggregate change in producers' surplus plus consumers' surplus: Change in the total of producers' surplus plus consumers' surplus has become the preferred basis of economists for measuring variations in social benefits as a result of the introduction of new agricultural techniques. It has been applied to the evaluation of green revolution technologies (Hayami & Herdt, 1985, Alauddin & Tisdell, 1986) and to the evaluation of weed control (Edwards & Freebairn, 1982; Auld, Menz, & Tisdell, 1987).

Wise (1978) has suggested, however, that to measure gains in producers' plus consumers' surplus is more demanding of information than measuring the total gain by estimating the cost reduction achieved by use of the new technique plus the size of stemming benefits. This method is illustrated in Figure 8.2.

In Figure 8.2, cost savings (on present production) are indicated by the hatched area, and stemming benefits are represented by the area of the dotted triangle. It might be noted that in many cases cost savings swamp stemming benefits as the prime social benefit from a new technique. Other things being equal, cost reductions are most likely to be much more significant than stemming benefits the larger the level of initial industry production, and then cost reductions will be a close approximation to the variation in total benefits. While this cost-side approach to evaluation does not provide information on the distribution of benefits between producers and consumers, variation in the distribution of benefits between these groups can be estimated if the variation in producers' surplus or alteration in

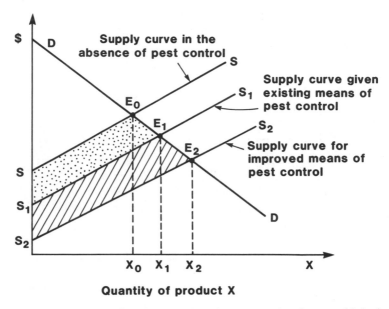

Figure 8.3 The benefits of new means of pest control such as new biological means must be evaluated relative to existing techniques of pest control.

consumers' surplus can be estimated, because change in consumers' surplus equals variation in total surplus less change in producers' surplus, and the variation in total surplus is known.

As was mentioned earlier, it is important to estimate the benefit of a new biological control technique in relation to the use of existing techniques. In Figure 8.3, SS represents the supply curve of product X in the absence of any control technique for a pest. With existing control techniques (say, based on pesticides), the supply curve is S_1S_1. With the introduction of biological control, the supply curve becomes S_2S_2. The social benefit from the biological control technique is as indicated by the hatched area and is *not* equal to the hatched area plus the dotted area. This means that the more cost-effective *nonbiological* techniques are, the smaller the social benefits from biological control are likely to be.

Note that variations in consumers' surplus plus producers' surplus in an industry will not be an adequate measure of social benefits when there are spillovers to other industries or when externalities beyond the industry occur from the use of classical biological controls. Such spillovers must be specifically taken into account (Industries Assistance Commission, 1985; Auld. et al., 1987, Ch. 8).

SOCIAL COST–BENEFIT ANALYSIS: SOME PITFALLS IN APPLYING IT TO BIOLOGICAL CONTROL

The above diagrammatic representations are only for a single period, but benefits, for example in terms of consumers' surplus, can be expected for several periods and will give rise to a stream of social net benefits. This has to be expressed in present value terms when using social cost–benefit analysis (Tisdell, 1972, Ch. 21; 1982, Sec. 17.7; Auld et al., 1987). If the present discounted value of outlays or investment in a biological control project is less than or equal to the present discounted value of social net benefits from the project, the project is worthwhile from a Kaldor–Hicks point of view. Alternatively, if

$$\frac{\text{discounted social net benefits}}{\text{discounted cost of project}}$$

$$= \frac{\text{discounted stream of change in consumers' plus producers' surplus}}{\text{discounted cost of project}}$$

$$= \frac{\text{discounted flow of cost savings plus stemming benefit}}{\text{discounted cost of project}}$$

$$> 1$$

the project passes the usual social cost–benefit test.

One should be careful to distinguish project costs from social losses arising from the project, otherwise social cost–benefit ratios computed may be misleading. This "error" was made by the Australian Industries Assistance Commission (IAC) in its inquiry into the possible biological control of *Echium* species (Tisdell, 1987a). It was noted that some groups of farmers would obtain increased profits from the biological control, whereas others would have their profits reduced. In the case considered, profit variations were an adequate measure of change in social net benefit. Let G represent the discounted increase in profit of the group gaining, and let L represent the discounted loss in profit of the group losing. Where P is the discounted cost of the project, the relevant benefit–cost ratio is $(G - L)/P$. But instead of using this ratio, the IAC used $G/(P + L)$, treating the losses to a group of farmers as a cost. To do so, however, is to understate the relative benefit of the project if the benefit–cost ratio exceeds 1. In the actual case considered by the IAC for the biological control of *Echium* species, *income losses* to groups of rural interests were estimated to be A\$13.4 million and research and implementation costs were expected to be A\$3.8 million giving a total cost according to IAC of A\$17.2 milliion (IAC, 1985, Ch. 7, p.8). Total benefits (income increases plus savings in control costs) were estimated to be A\$148.5 million. Using the formula $G/(P + L)$ as used by the IAC, the benefit–cost ratio is 8.6/1. However, using the more defensible formula $(G - L)/P$, the benefit–cost ratio is 35.6/1. Thus benefit–cost ratios can be seriously underestimated if the incorrect formula is used, as this case illustrates. If the Kaldor–Hicks rule is adopted, there is no justification for treating the loss of one group of farmers as a project cost.

Turning to a slightly different point which also emphasizes the need for care, Wise (1978) claims that several empirical studies, including that of Griliches (1957) on hybrid corn, overstate the returns to research and development because these fail to include *all* relevant items in the project costs—especially investments required downstream to take advantage of the technology.

Clearly the evaluation of a potential biological control of a pest can be a complex matter even from an economic viewpoint and limiting oneself to traditional social cost–benefit analysis. But the question is even more complicated than this, for account also needs to be taken of its consequences for income distribution, for variability or instability of benefits, its implications for sustainability of economic processes, as well as uncertainty. The evaluation problem thus is not single-dimensional but multidimensional (cf. Conway, 1987; Tisdell, 1988b).

FUTURE SCOPE FOR BIOLOGICAL PEST CONTROL

Even if we only consider classical biological pest control, biological control has had a major favorable economic impact, and social economic returns from research into and implementation of biological control programmes have been high (Tisdell, 1988a, 1989). Nevertheless, expenditure on research into and development of chemical pesticides in comparison to that for biological control is about 8.5/1 (Huffaker, Simmonds, & Laing, 1976, pp. 66–67). This may reflect the greater ability of companies or businesses to *appropriate* benefits from toxicological research compared to biological research in this area, rather than much higher social benefits from toxicological research (Tisdell et al., 1984).

Whether the degree of economic success that has been achieved with classical biological control in the past is likely to be maintained in future efforts remains uncertain. Some scientists suggest no appreciable tapering off in the application of these methods. For instance, Wilson and Huffaker (1976, p. 6) say that "enormous resources of natural enemies exist and the research possibilities for [biological] pest control are virtually unlimited." DeBach (1974, p. 195) claims that "despite the substantial progress that has been made in the field of biological control there is no doubt that its application could be greatly increased." On the other hand, the findings of Julien et al. (1984) suggest some tapering off in the effectiveness of biological releases for weed control. They point out that while there has been a marked increase in the number of attempts of biological control of weeds with the lapse of time, effectiveness decreased from 36 percent of all releases between 1940 and 1949 to 14 percent between 1970 and 1979.

Furthermore, it would be unwise to ignore the possible adverse implications for biological control of reduced species diversity due (1) to the global disappearance of species, and (2) the increased geographical translocation and mixing of species (biological entropy) due mainly to the activities of man. Such factors may make it more difficult to sustain economic returns from the biological control reliant on the *import* of natural enemies. This does not provide grounds for being pessimistic about future economic prospects for all forms of biological control of insects and weeds, even though these prospects are dependent upon the global preservation of an adequate array of biological resources.

Control methods involving augmentation, conservation of natural enemies, or inundation appear to have been relatively underexplored, and there is room for optimism about their economic prospects, relying, for instance, on the use of pathogens, selective breeding, improved cultural practices, and genetic manipulation. As the relative importance of nonclassical methods of biological control is likely to grow, much more economic research into these is needed. With the passage of time we may come to appreciate more fully the valuable role played by natural enemies in controlling pests, and by adequate care of these natural resources we may obtain more effective, sustainable, and economic pest control. It is important both in the economic growth process and in the use of modern technologies that we do not accidentally eliminate the natural enemies of pests, for this can be to our long-run economic cost and that of future generations.

9

Rural–Urban Migration, Population, and Labor Allocation: Labor Surplus Models and Alternatives

Rural–urban migration, population growth, and the regional allocation of labor are important aspects of economic development, with significant implications for the growth of per capita income and for the state of the environment. Today the developed regions of the world are largely urbanized, with just over 70 percent of the population of these regions estimated to live in urban areas (World Commission on Environment and Development, 1987, p. 236). In less developed countries, on the other hand, the urban–rural mix of the population is reversed, with just over 30 percent of the population estimated to live in urban areas (ibid.). Nevertheless, in the last three decades the urbanization of LDCs has been occurring at a rapid pace, so that many megacities now exist in Third World countries. But few city governments in the developing world are able to cope with such rapid urban growth, and as a result essential infrastructure is often inadequate, and the unhealthy environments that have developed have become the source of disease and international concern (World Commission on Environment and Development, 1987, Ch. 9).

Many theories of economic development imply, however, that industrialization and urbanization provide the most promising means for Third World countries to achieve economic growth. This is true, for example, of the classical theory of economic development based on labor surplus and expounded by Lewis (1954, 1965, 1979). But such theories tend to emphasize the benefits of industrialization and to ignore the drawbacks—especially the environmental ones (Ekins, 1986, p. 36).

Lewis argued that there is a labor surplus in agriculture, and that this can be most productively absorbed by the expansion of manufacturing industry, which in normal circumstances implies an increase in urbanization. (For easily readable reviews see Ranis & Fei, 1982; Little, 1982.) Indeed, Lewis went so far as to suggest that there is so much labor in agriculture and in the rural sector that its marginal productivity is zero in agriculture (even negative in some cases). Thus it was believed that manufacturing production could be expanded by absorbing labor from the rural sector *without* a loss in rural production. Furthermore, Lewis (1954) argued that a virtually unlimited supply of labor (a perfectly elastic supply of labor) may be available from the subsistence sector to support manufacturing growth. This can occur either because the existing rural labor surplus involves such a large available pool or because rural population increases quickly if rural income per capita tends to rise above subsistence level as a result of any outflow of labor to urban areas. Basically, the economic salvation of LDCs is seen in the expansion of the manufacturing sector and urbanization, and policies to encourage capital formation in manufacturing are favored.

LEWIS, RANIS, AND FEI REVISITED

Lewis (1954) assumed dual labor markets, in the sense that the real wage rate in manufacturing is supposed to be an institutionally determined constant wage rate in excess of the per capita income of laborers in the agricultural sector (the agricultural population). If we suppose that, at least, in the short run, the total labor force in the economy is given, an economy of the Lewis type may be in an initial position as depicted in Figure 9.1, with L_A*** of the labor force engaged in agriculture and L_M* employed in manufacturing. Income per capita in the agriculture sector is w*, and the institutionally determined wage rate in the manufacturing sector is w***. (In practice, Lewis thought that capitalist wages, even in long-term

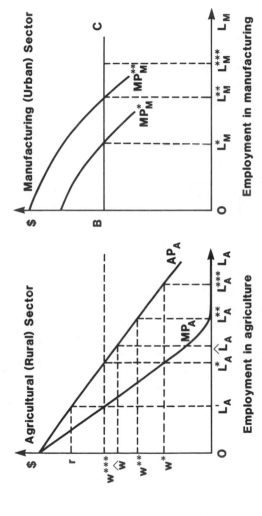

Figure 9.1 A simplified version of the Lewis-type labor surplus model.

equilibrium, might remain about 30 percent higher than subsistence earnings. However, this gap is ignored in the analysis presented here.)

Suppose now that the marginal product curve of labor in the manufacturing sector shifts from that identified by MP_M^* to that indicated by MP_M^{**}, say due to investment in manufacturing. The equilibrium quantity of labor employed in manufacturing rises from L_M^* to L_M^{**}, and the extra supply can be found by withdrawing $L_A^{***} - L_A^{**}$ of labor from the agricultural sector. Since the marginal productivity of labor in agriculture in zero, total agricultural production remains unaltered, and income per head in the agricultural sector rises from w^* to w^{**}. The income of the bulk of the population rises, assuming that the labor force remains constant.

Ranis and Fei (1961) pointed out that productivity or efficiency gains from labor relocation by sectors is not dependent on the marginal productivity of labor in agriculture being zero. Provided that the latter is lower than in manufacturing, gains in production can be made by shifting labor to manufacturing. Thus if, say, initially L_A of labor is employed in agriculture, total production could be increased by reallocating $\hat{L}_A - L_A^*$ of labor to manufacturing.

In the model illustrated by Figure 9.1, long-term equilibrium is achieved when income per capita in agriculture is equal to the institutionally determined wage rate in manufacturing. This occurs when L_A^* of labor is allocated to agriculture and L_M^{***} is employed in manufacturing. The length of time required to reach this equilibrium is dependent on the strength of investment in manufacturing, which shifts the marginal physical productivity curve of labor upwards there. Indeed, if investment in manufacturing does not grow sufficiently, the gap between the wage rate in manufacturing and income per head in agriculture will not be closed.

Tisdell and T. I. Fairbairn (1984) pointed out that in an equilibrium in which the average product of labor in agriculture or rural areas is equated to its marginal product in manufacturing or in urban areas, total production is not maximized in relation to the given labor force. More labor is retained in the rural sector than is optimal from the point of view of maximizing production in the economy as a whole.

In the case illustrated in Figure 9.1, production is maximized when the marginal physical productivity of labor in agriculture equals that in manufacturing or urban areas. Given that BC is the effective curve of marginal productivity of labor in manufacturing, overall production is maximized when only L'_A of labor is retained agriculture in the rural sector and the remainder allocated in the long term to manufacturing or the urban sector. Such an equilibrium would not come about if a traditional income-sharing system applies in rural society *and rent is absent.* Tisdell and Fairbairn (ibid.) indicate some societies in which these conditions may be approximated. *If* the goal in such a society is to maximize aggregate income, then this might be achieved by imposing a per capita tax on rural sector income (per person) equivalent to $(r - w^{***})$ in the case shown in Figure 9.1, or providing a subsidy for movement to the urban sector *once* the equilibrium is approached.

Yotopolous and Nugent (1976) argue that the above type of rural labor surplus theories deal with largely irrelevant issues, since urban areas do not have a labor shortage but a labor surplus, reflected in urban unemployment and underemployment. However, it could be argued that the situation being observed is a disequilibrium one: Individuals have been enticed to urban areas from rural ones by the *prospect* of obtaining a higher income, but to find a position in the urban environment takes time, and the increased availability of urban jobs depends on the level of investment on manufacturing (or other urban-based industry).

This is not to suggest that "labor surplus" theories are without problems. Meier (1964, Sec. 11.5) and Basu (1984) indicate some of these: manufacturing and urban-based industry requires to a large extent skilled or semi-skilled labor, and a large pool of this is not available from rural areas (cf. Barber, 1961). Furthermore, the demand for manufacturing production is not considered in a general equilibrium framework. Indeed, one of the weaknesses of the simple theories of labor surplus economies is their failure to give in-depth attention to the interdependence of sectors in the economy, in terms both of demand and of input requirements (see Maitra, 1988c; Kelley, Williamson, & Cheetham, 1972; Jorgenson,

1967; Fei & Ranis, 1964). However, the presumption of such theories that returns to investment are highest in manufacturing (or urban-located industry) and zero or very low in agriculture would appear to be a most important one and central to the policy advice that has been based on these theories in the past. Taking especially the development of technologies associated with the Green Revolution into account, this presumption has not always been justified (see, for example, Chaudhri & Dasgupta, 1985, Ch. 2).

ALLOWING FOR REMITTANCES AND EXTENDED FAMILY DECISION-MAKING

In considering labor movements or migration from rural to urban areas, attention needs to be given to remittances and, in many developing countries, the importance of the extended family in decision-making involving migration (in the latter respect, see Sathiendrakumar & Tisdell, 1987). Tisdell and T. I. Fairbairn (1984) point out that in traditional sharing societies remittances from family relatives in urban centers to family members in rural areas may help retain labor in agriculture or rural areas, thereby reducing the supply of labor for manufacturing or urban occupation. In that model, it was assumed that family migration from rural to urban areas would proceed to the point where income per head for family members in the urban area after payment of remittances is equal to that for rural family members after receipt of remittances. This is a myopic adjustment that, in effect, equalizes averages.

While this model is not implausible, another possibility may also exist: a conscious decision may be made by the head or leadership of the extended family to maximize the overall income of the extended family. This requires that family members be allocated or *directed* to areas so that their marginal contribution to extended family income is equal in all areas. Discrepancies in average or overall income in different areas can then be smoothed out by the family through income transfers. Under the conditions discussed so far, *such a system will maximize total production and lead to the most efficient allocation of labor*. But it does require direction of family members rather than relatively short-sighted responses on their part to signals. Only empirical evidence can help us to choose between competing models in terms of relevance to actual situations.

The study of extended family influences on labor movement and migration would seem to be important in understanding the forces at work in many developing countries. But it should be added that changes in location are not influenced solely by pecuniary motives, even within an extended family. An extended family may have its roots in a rural setting, and it may be from there that its leaders or elders derive their power and status. This may mean that utility functions for the extended family are biased in favor of maintaining a base in the rural area—at least, this is likely to be so initially, as family members migrate to urban areas. However, eventually it is possible for the base to alter from the country to the city, once the extended family has become sufficently established in the urban area.

RENT AND THE OPTIMAL ALLOCATION OF LABOR

Neoclassical economists have, on the whole, tended to see rent and private property as having a socially useful purpose in bringing about an efficient allocation of resources, whereas classical economists did not see rent and the landlord's claims in such a benign light. This, however, raises the question of whether the payment of rent in agriculture will promote an optimal allocation of labor between rural and urban areas.

Indeed, given the simple model considered in relation to Figure 9.1, land rent would help to bring about such an allocation. While the equilibrium suggested by Tisdell and T. I. Fairbairn (1984) prevails in a sharing society in which landlords are absent, the presence of landlords alters the situation. Sharing may be a characteristic of the tribal or clan-type societies of some Pacific islands or of parts of Africa; it may even be typical of some feudal societies. But it is debatable whether this is characteristic of India and other Asian countries, where rental payments for the use of land are not uncommon, even though according to Little (1982, p. 91) Lewis "thought his theory applied mainly to Asia [and Egypt]." When landlords are present in agriculture, the effect is that instead of L_A^*

of labor being retained (in the absence of remittances), only L'_A of labor is retained. Landlords take $(r - w^{***})\, L'_A$ in rental or impose a rental payment of $(r - w^{***})$ for each person employed. Thereby, the marginal productivity of labor in agriculture is, in equilibrium, brought into equality with that in manufacturing. The same effect is achieved as would be achieved by the government tax on employment in agriculture (or subsidy to that in manufacturing), as mentioned above.

However, while rent may ensure efficiency in the allocation of those employed, it may fail to maximize production in relation to the level of population. It will do this if it supports an idle class. This can be readily appreciated. Suppose that the rental income illustrated in Figure 9.1 supports in equilibrium a landlord class of population size P, which is idle and serves no productive function. By adding this group to the workforce in manufacturing, an increase in output of $w^{***}P = DB.P$ can be obtained, and the efficiency condition can still be satisfied. Thus the efficiency argument in itself is not a compelling one on productivity grounds in favor of landlords obtaining pure rent.

AN EXTENDED SHARING OF INCOME MODEL

It may be of interest to extend the Tisdell and Fairbairn (1984) income-sharing model to sharing within urban areas, in addition to sharing in rural areas. In some countries, rural families, when they settle in urban areas, continue to share income among family there. If we suppose no remittances and rents in this extended model, in equilibrium labor is allocated between locations so as to equalize per capita income at each location.

If we suppose that diminishing marginal productivity of labor at each location is the rule and if the average product curve of labor differs at different locations, more labor will be allocated to the most productive area than required to maximize aggregate production. This is in accordance with the proposition of Gordon (1954) in relation to common property or common-access resources. Thus if the urban area is the relatively more productive area, in equilibrium more labor will be allocated to the urban area and less to the rural area than is necessary to maximize production. The urban area, and employment there, will be overexpanded (cf. Tisdell, 1975).

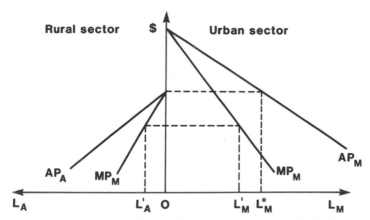

Rural sector $ **Urban sector**

AP_A MP_M MP_M AP_M

L_A L'_A O L'_M L^*_M L_M

Employment in agriculture   Employment in manufacturing sector

Figure 9.2 Illustration of a model in which rural–urban labor movements are based on average incomes or productivity rather than marginal productivity. This may occur due to income sharing arrangements between social groups such as extended families in some societies.

This may be illustrated by Figure 9.2. In this case, under extended averaging, all the available labor L_M^* is allocated to the urban area, given the same interpretation of the curves shown as presented earlier. But the most efficient allocation is that which maximizes aggregate output and equalizes the marginal product of labor in urban and rural areas. In the case illustrated, this occurs when L'_A of the available labor is allocated to rural areas and L'_M is allocated to urban employment. Of course, if rural industry is relatively more productive than urban, the bias in labor allocation would run the other way.

DUAL URBAN LABOR MARKETS AND URBAN UNEMPLOYMENT AND UNDEREMPLOYMENT

There is considerable evidence to suggest that in developing countries dual labor markets exist in urban areas, not just between agriculture and manufacturing. Outlets for small-scale self-employment and casual employment in urban areas co-exist with more formal possibilities for employment. Income per head of those engaged in informal employment may be much lower than in rural areas. But, along the lines of the theory suggested by Todaro (1969), individuals may migrate from rural areas to urban areas because this increases their *probability* of (eventually) finding employment in the higher-paying more formal labor market in the urban area, thereby substantially raising their expected level of income. In Todaro's model, the rate of rural to urban migration depends upon several factors, including the degree of unemployment in urban areas and the differences in the levels of income between rural and urban areas. Clearly, the existence of the informal sector in the urban environment also acts as an attractant to would-be rural emigrants since, as a "halfway house," it provides prospects of some income while waiting for employment in the formal urban sector. Sharing of income may also be a common feature in this sector.

Writers such as Todaro have suggested that present procedures in LDCs for finding jobs for migrants to cities are economically wasteful, since they result in a large pool of unemployed and underemployed individuals in cities. He has suggested (Todaro, 1971) that migration to cities should be restricted. Under his proposed scheme, "all employment openings are channelled through [government-run urban] labor exchanges and allocated among the potential migrants, who are registered by lot" (Yotopoulos & Nugent, 1976, p. 230).

But this raises the question of how efficient a government agency is likely to be in job placement, given some differences in skills required and qualities of laborers. Furthermore, it might be argued that some period of residency in an urban environment, even if unemployed or underemployed, is useful in adapting rural emigrants to city life and requirements, as they learn by doing or by being present. This is not to deny that in a disequilibrium situation of common access to the city more individuals may migrate to the city than is economically efficient and that some measures may be in order to curtail the extent of the flow. However, it is one thing to say this and another to argue that the flow should be stemmed to such an extent that urban unemployment and underemployment disappear.

Models dealing with the optimal allocation of labor in LDCs clearly raise a number of fundamental issues that are still not resolved. As for standard classical and neoclassical models of labor allocation, Yotopolous and Nugent (1976) are skeptical about their value, pointing out that neoclassical economic theory suggests that differential rates of return to labor should eventually be eliminated by migration. They say that migration "flows have been incapable of decreasing, let alone of eliminating rural–urban income differentials," and dualism has often become more widespread (Yotopolous & Nugent, 1976, p. 220). In this regard, Sathiendrakumar and Tisdell (1987) found evidence indicating that migration increases income disparities in fishing villages in the Maldives, with its poorest families being relatively most disadvantaged. However, it should be emphasized that the neoclassical contention is that *eventually* income differentials will disappear. The adjustment mechanism is not specified, and the *possibility* is allowed that things could become worse before they become better. It is possible that Yotopolos and Nugents' critique is primarily a criticism of the use of the method of comparative statics as applied to this subject and used for policy prescriptions.

Theorizing about a subject such as economic development by depending on a simplified model is bound to be inadequate. But some points of reference, however primitive, are needed for discussion purposes, even though they may mirror reality poorly. Furthermore, phenomena such as dualism in LDCs may have several causes, as may its magnifications, which are not captured at all by labor surplus models (cf. Meier, 1964, ch. 2).

It might be observed that in most labor surplus models the manufacturing sector and the urban sector are taken to be synonymous. But of course this leaves out the significance of tertiary industry in the urban environment. In some LDCs manufacturing is relatively unimportant, but urban areas continue to grow by reliance on tertiary industry, especially the government sector. This is particularly important, for example, in relation to small, less developed island countries in the Pacific, where cash income is mostly dependent on government sector employment (Bertram, 1986; Connell, 1986).

RESUME OF BASIC LEWIS' PROPOSITIONS AND SOME FURTHER ISSUES

The Lewis model assumes that the drift of labor to rural areas depends on capital formation in urban areas and is closely attuned to such formation, so substantial urban unemployment does not occur. The movement of labor to urban areas is seen as adding to economic efficiency, since there capital in combination with labor is considered to be more productive than in rural areas. The actual exposition of the theory is reliant on comparative statics, and, as indicated previously, labor supply to urban areas just keeps pace with demand in this model.

In the Lewis model, if population is constant, the proportion of the population at the subsistence wage falls. If the subsistence wage represents an absolute poverty level, the number of individuals in absolute poverty falls. But initially income inequality can increase. In the long term, however, as capital formation proceeds in urban areas, wage rates in urban and rural areas should tend to equality. Thus the theory suggests that over time inequality of (wage) income will tend to follow the pattern suggested by Kuznets (1963)—that is, at first increasing with economic development and then declining.

We have already noted a number of shortcomings of the theory. It has also been pointed out that although wage inequality would (virtually) disappear in the Lewis model in the long term, production from the amount of labor employed in the economy as a whole is not at a maximum. This occurs if labor is paid its average product in rural areas but its marginal product in urban areas.

Another significant feature that has not been taken into account is the possibility of increasing returns to regional production up to a point as a result of increased population in a particular area or region. If population movements occur in response to average (or expected) income levels, this can result in population movements and settlements that do not lead to production being maximized relative to employed labor.

Such a situation can result in population centers becoming too large to maximize production relative to the labor force and to the failure of settlements to grow at the most productive sites (cf. Tisdell, 1975; Richardson, 1978). This can be illustrated by two simple examples:

Suppose that two sites are available for settlement and that the average product curves of population at these two sites, A and B, are as indicated in Figure 9.3 by the curves marked DEF and HJK. Suppose that due to historical accident population tends at first to settle at site A rather than site B. Average product and income per

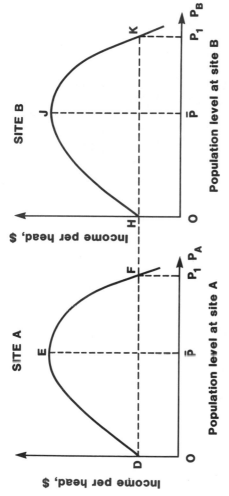

Figure 9.3 Failure of the population or the labor force to maximize production in relation to available resources because population moves myopically in response to differences in (average) income per head between sites.

capita at site A exceeds that at site B, and, assuming myopic adjustment, the settlement at site A expands, whereas there is no settlement at site B until population reaches P_1 at site A. At any population greater than P_1 the settlement at site B will grow at the expense of A, and if total population is less then $2P_1$ both settlements will be too small in equilibrium to maximize production. Thus as population increases, there may be a shift from a situation where settlement A is over large to one where both settlements are too small from an economic efficiency viewpoint.

In addition, at any time there may be failure of a region or area to grow because at low levels of population average product there is lower than elsewhere, but at higher population levels its average product may be higher than in more densely populated areas. Hence, total production is less than can be achieved. This can be illustrated by Figure 9.4. Once again assume two sites A and B for simplicity. Let curve DEF represent the average product of population region A and HJK indicate that in region B. Suppose that a population P_0 has settled in region A. If this population were transferred to region B, income per head would rise and total product in relation to population would rise, as can be appreciated by inspection of Figure 9.4. To the extent that economies of scale in relation to settlement sites are important, we do need to find ways to incorporate these specifically into the analysis of rural–urban labor movements. Indications are that much more development of the relevant theory of this subject is needed.

In practice, there are further problems that need adequate explanation (not at present provided by traditional theory) as far as population movements are concerned. In the United States, at least, differences in per capita incomes between regions seem to persist for decades despite population movements, and incomes per capita in the different regions tend to grow at the same rate, according to recent evidence discussed by Mao (1988), who provides a theoretical explanation of this phenomenon.

The neoclassical theory of labor employment suggests that an optimal allocation of labor between regions automatically comes about if there are no constraints on labor movements, and that wages for labor of the same quality tend to equality everywhere. But this is not so in the situations shown in Figures 9.3 and 9.4, and it is not in accordance with a number of observations such as the

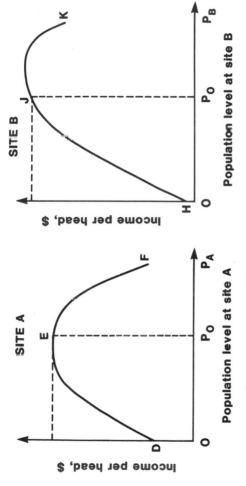

Figure 9.4 Persistent but suboptimal economic growth of a site where growth was once optimal but is no longer so once the overall level of population exceeds some threshold level.

persistence of income inequalities just mentioned. The classical labor surplus model of Lewis (1954) also ignores economies of urban agglomeration and misdirected urban development due to responses to current conditions (that is, adaptive behavior involving localized responses). Furthermore, it only predicts a limited increase in inequality of income with economic development, increasing inequality ultimately giving way to falling inequality in distribution of income. By contrast, center–periphery theories of economic development suggest that economic growth of urban centers or central regions may lead to increasing inequalities in income between regions and that "trickle-down" of economic benefits may fail to occur in less developed regions when growth centers develop (Ekins, 1986, Ch. 1; Tisdell, 1982, Sec. 18.4). Indeed, most center–periphery theorists go further and argue that economic disadvantages are likely to accrue to less developed regions or to peripheral areas as a result of the development of economic centers, whether within a country or internationally. For example, the development of centers on the coastal region of China could lead to economic drawbacks for the less developed Western regions, and the further development of the more developed countries of the world could be to the economic disadvantage of the less developed countries. Thus there are a number of competing economic theories or paradigms in this area of economic development. However, all tend to ignore the environmental consequences of the development of economic centers that involve urbanization and industrialization.

THE ENVIRONMENT, URBANIZATION, AND INDUSTRIALIZATION OF THE THIRD WORLD

While economic theories such as those of Lewis tend to emphasize urbanization and industrialization as the economic way forward for less developed countries, the difficulties that LDCs face on pursuing this path have been underrated. Apart from the difficulties that many LDCs find in competing internationally in marketing industrial goods because the (internal) domestic markets of many LDCs are too small to support extensive secondary industry (given economies of scale in manufacturing, most would be forced to depend on exports for economic viability of such industries), most Third World countries face major environmental problems in urbanizing and industrializing.

Urbanization and industrialization generally lead to the concentration of wastes in a locality—that is, wastes from economic production as well as waste from humans, such as sewage. Because of this concentration, natural ecological processes are as a rule unable to cope with the degradation of these wastes. This requires artificial means to be used to supplement natural processes, e.g. sewage treatment works and greater regulation of the emission of wastes, otherwise human health is likely to suffer and economic production may be adversely affected by environmental spillovers or externalities. For example, water may become unfit for either domestic or industrial use, and many living organisms in the water such as fish may perish or be contaminated.

In China, for example, there are complaints that urban and industrial expansion is having an adverse impact on agricultural production. For instance, authorities in Hebei Province complain that effluent from Beijing and from Tianjin is adding to the cost of water treatment in that province. In Hubei Province, the release of pollutants from a factory in Sashi City (near Wuhan) into a canal is reported to have killed livestock, made the water unsuitable for irrigation by farmers downstream, ruined agricultural land for cropping use in areas where the water has been applied in the past for irrigation, and adversely affected human health. In Shanghai, widespread and serious outbreaks of hepatitis are largely attributable to sewage disposal problems (Nickum & Dixon, 1989). As stated by the World Commission on Environment and Development (1987, p. 238):

Few city governments in the developing world have the power, resources and trained staff to provide their rapidly growing populations with the land, services, and facilities needed for an adequate human life: clean water, sanitation, schools and transport.

Environmental factors need to be taken into account in the planning of urban developments and in determining optimum locations, size, and rates of growth of urban areas.

Urban concentration may also adversely affect the recycling of wastes that could maintain the fertility of the soil and its structure.

In China, for example, declining soil fertility has been attributed to declining use and recycling of organic waste (including nightsoil) in agriculture with the growth of cities. The cost of transporting such wastes to the countryside in comparison to the use of artificial fertilizers (often subsidized by government) may have become too high. Nickum and Dixon (1989, p. 90) point out that many Chinese farmers have changed to chemical fertilizers; they state that "these may not provide the long-term benefits to the soil structure that organic fertilizers would, but they do provide many of the key nutrients such as nitrogen in a cleaner, more convenient way." Nevertheless, this does not imply that their increasing use is socially optimal. Account needs to be taken of the impact on the environment of chemical fertilizers and their consequences for the sustainability of agricultural production. Ideally, ecological problems of this nature should be taken into account in planning urban development.

Industrialization and urbanization of the Third World can be expected to create environmental problems for the whole world if it is associated with increased energy use, as seems likely. It is estimated for example, that if energy consumption per head were to become uniform throughout the world by 2025 at per capita levels now prevailing in industrial countries, this would involve an increase in total energy use per year of more than five times the total energy use in 1980 (World Commission on Environment and Development, 1987, p. 175). While an increase to this extent in per capita energy consumption in LDCs is unlikely by 2025, substantial increases in energy consumption from fossil fuels in the Third World will increase the serious likelihood of climatic change resulting from the greenhouse effect, increase urban air pollution, raise the prevalence of acid rains and acidification, and add to environmental problems and risks. Even if much of this extra energy is generated by nuclear means, there will still be additional environmental risks. The developed world cannot ignore the environmental impact of the urbanization and industrialization of the Third World, given the environmental global interdependence of the modern world. This is one of the reasons why it has become more urgent to address environmental, ecological, and economic issues such as those raised in publications like *Our Common Future* (World Commission on Environment and Development, 1987).

CONCLUDING COMMENT

This chapter has shown that in relation to *equilibrium* situations, a labor surplus may—but need not—exist in agriculture, given the simplest framework for the labor surplus models. Some conditions under which a surplus or a deficit of labor would exist in agriculture or rural areas have been specified.

Disequilibrium situations are very much more difficult to model than those in equilibrium, since such a variety of reaction mechanisms are possible. But even when a labor surplus exists in agriculture (in rural areas), it is possible for rural–urban migration to proceed faster than is optimal from a scarcity-reducing point of view. It is possible for urban unemployment and underemployment in a dynamic setting to be too great. On the other hand, it may be optimal to tolerate *some* urban unemployment and underemployment, insofar as it forms part of the search, learning, and adjustment process for rural emigrants. This is not to suggest that a callous attitude should be taken to urban unemployment and underemployment in LDCs, nor that improved adjustment mechanisms should not be sought.

Traditional economic development models favoring industrialization and urbanization as development policies for the Third World have tended to ignore the environmental and ecological consequences of such policies. These cannot be realistically ignored in the modern world because economic and ecological variables are interdependent. Urbanization may still be a desirable policy for the Third World, but its speed if not its nature may need to be modified by ecological and environmental considerations. As is apparent from *Our Common Future* (World Commission on Environment and Development, 1987, Ch. 8), a more sophisticated approach to industrialization and development policies is needed than has been used in the past.

10

Foreign Assistance to Resource-poor Developing Countries: Aid versus International Migration

Small developing island economies in the Pacific, many of which are atoll economies and most of which are resource-poor, have their per capita income levels maintained significantly by foreign aid from donor countries such as Australia, New Zealand, the United States, France, and other countries (Bertram & Watters, 1985, 1986; Bertram, 1986; Fairbairn, 1985, Ch. 5). Bertram and Watters (1985), drawing on New Zealand's interrelationship with many of these economies, describe these as MIRAB (Migration, Remittances, Aid, Bureaucracy) or even MIRAG economies (if the word government is substituted for bureaucracy). They claim that their model of these economies as a whole and its elements (Mi: migration, R: remittances, A: aid financed, B: bureaucracy) direct attention to a relatively new and largely exogenous set of factors that do not merely supplement onshore commodity production in the islands but have increasingly and decisively dominated the respective island economies and largely determined their evolution (Bertram & Watters, 1986, p. 47). Economies such as those of the Cook Islands, Niue, and Tokelau are heavily dependent on migration to New Zealand, on remittances from their emigrants, and on foreign aid from New Zealand (and similar countries), which is

mostly used to support a large government bureaucracy or government sector. The government sector is virtually the only cash
income sector for these economies.

On the other hand, several small economies in the Pacific are
without significant or permanent outlets for migration. This is
particularly so in the case of Kiribati and Tuvalu. Although
Bertram (1986) does describe Kiribati and Tuvalu as MIRAB
economies, this seems inappropriate. According to the statistics
quoted by Bertram (ibid., p. 813), the Cook Islands, Niue, and
Tokelau had, respectively, 44, 61, and 45 percent of their island-
born population in New Zealand, Kiribati had only 4 percent
overseas and Tuvalu 11 percent. Most of the latter are employed in
phosphate mining in Nauru, and mining there is expected to cease
in the near future. Kiribati and Tuvalu are best described as AB
(Aid, Bureaucracy) economies. In AB economies, as in MIRAB
economies, aid is funneled principally into the public sector, and it
is the principal source of cash income. Bertram (ibid.) and others
also suggest that this type of aid may encourage the growth of
capital cities or main islands in these economies and the depopulation of outer islands and lead to a decline in production by traditional industries—for example, through the effect of the so-called
Dutch disease (van Wijnbergen, 1984). However, this matter is not
analyzed here. Rather, it is taken for granted that the main purpose
of foreign aid to small island developing nations (SINS) in the
Pacific is to maintain income through cash payments for employment in the public sector. In the first instance, this aid will be
regarded as a means of income transfer rather than a payment for
production. Bertram (1986, p. 812) provides statistics to show that
the major portion of government expenditure in Tokelau, Kiribati,
and Tuvalu is financed by foreign aid, and more than one-third of
such expenditure in the Cook Islands and Niue is similarly financed.
He emphasizes that the bulk of each government's budget is spent
on wages and salaries for the provision of modern services to the
population, so that the expenditure of external budgetary assistance generates two rounds of improvement to living standard in the
islands: government services in the first round, and private consumption out of cash income in the second (ibid., p. 812).

Here we shall consider alternative policies that might be adopted
or considered by a donor country *to minimize its foreign aid bill to a*

SIN, assuming that it wishes to maintain per capita income in the SIN at a target level above that achievable by the SIN on the basis of its own resources and given its level of population.[1] It should be noted that aspects of our policy discussion have relevance also to resource-poor LDCs that are not small island nations. Emphasis will be placed on population control as a policy—particularly the possibility of emigration to the donor country. For instance, migration is an option that Australia can consider in relation to Kiribati and Tuvalu, which has been recommended by some researchers (Ward, 1986). Others, on the other hand, oppose migration because of possible adverse economic and social/cultural impact on SINS (Connell, 1986). Connell points out that the Compact of Free Association between various Micronesian states and the United States could result in Micronesian residents of the United States outnumbering "the folks back home." He goes on to say, "this situation already exists in Niue, Tokelau and the Cook Islands and presents a future for atoll states that has nothing to do with self-reliance and which is received with concern and disarray by many in these countries" (ibid., p. 49).

Simple production models will be used to analyze the possible impact of population control, especially migration, on per capita income[2] in a SIN. The consequences of three variants of the production function—namely, decreasing returns, constant returns, and increasing returns followed by diminishing returns, as associated with the views of Ricardo, Mellor, and Marshall, respectively—will be considered, leading on to a discussion of investment and technology transfer as alternatives to population control and further discussion of policy, and subsequently to economic and environmental sustainability issues.

THE BASIC PRODUCTION MODEL AND AIM

Let us suppose that the aggregate income available to a SIN depends only on its population level, that is,

$$Y = f(P) \tag{1}$$

where Y is aggregate income or output and P represents its population level. Assume also that a donor wishes to maintain per capita income in the SIN at a level a or greater. Thus there is a condition to satisfy:

$$Y/P \geq a \qquad (2)$$

This constraint will be satisfied for a value of Y of T or greater where

$$T = aP \qquad (3)$$

The problem is to minimize the foreign aid transfer S required to achieve the target income, given that S is being used merely to fill the gap between the target and locally produced income. Mathematically the problem is to minimize

$$S = T - f(P)$$
$$= aP - f(P) \qquad (4)$$

where P is regarded as a controlled variable, either most realistically through emigration or less realistically via birth control.

In addition, a further constraint or constraints may be relevant. The donor may not wish to depopulate a SIN completely. Clearly, complete depopulation will result in aid requirements of zero; but for strategic, political, and sympathetic reasons the donor may decide to minimize S subject to $P \geq P^*$ where P^* is positive.

Different forms of the production function $f(P)$ have different implications for the impact of emigration from a SIN on the foreign aid supplement needed to achieve the target level of per capita income. Let us consider in turn production functions as suggested by Ricardo, Mellor, and Marshall.

THE RICARDIAN CASE: DECREASING RETURNS

In the Ricardian case (Ricardo, 1817), diminishing returns apply, so $f''(P) < 0$. If we assume that marginal product is positive, $f'(P) > 0$, two cases can be distinguished: (a) $f(P)$ lies entirely below the target line, (b) $f(P)$ intersects the target line from above. These are illustrated in Figures 10.1 and 10.2, respectively.

Consider case (a) as illustrated in Figure 10.1. In this case, no level of domestic production can be achieved by the SIN that will enable the target level of income to be satisfied. However, as the level of population of the SIN is reduced, per capita income rises, and the required amount of the total foreign aid subsidy S falls. For example, if the current level of population of the SIN is P_3, a foreign aid amount of AB is required, but if population is reduced to P_2, aid equivalent to only CD is needed to match the target. In this case, the donor has an interest in seeing the population of the SIN reduced to the lowest acceptable level, P^*.

Consider now case (b), as illustrated in Figure 10.2. If the population of the SIN is such that aid is required to reach the target income level, reduction of population to a positive level (P_2 in the case illustrated) enables the target to be met without aid. For example, if population is reduced from P_3 to P_2, aid can be reduced from AB per period to zero. This supposes, of course, that $P^* < P_2$. If $P^* > P_2$, the same type of solution applies as in the previous case.

This simple rendition assumes that population reduction has no impact on the production function and that aid is also neutral in this respect and takes no account of possible remittances by emigrants from SINS.[3] It is theoretically consistent with a reduction in population brought about by migration of a representative profile of the community in terms of age structure, skill structure, and so on and assumes that no remittances are made by this group.

If remittances are made, the income gap to be filled by the donor will be lower than otherwise, and, in addition, emigrants should add to production in the donor country.[4] On the other hand, if the more productive members of the community emigrate, this will tend to move the production function downward in the SIN. So account should be taken of any variation in home production on account of a reduction of the population and of a change in the composition of the population, as well as remittances by emigrants.

Birth control may be an alternative to emigration as a means of population control, but it takes considerable time to have an impact and not all sectors of the community may be supportive of it. Until one comes to a new stationary equilibrium, the age profile of the population remains unbalanced, so an impact on the production function can be expected.

Whether or not decreasing returns as a function of population size are typical for SINS is difficult to say a priori, but it does not seem an unrealistic possibility for some mini-SINS in the Pacific; for some of these the situation in Figure 10.1 could even apply.

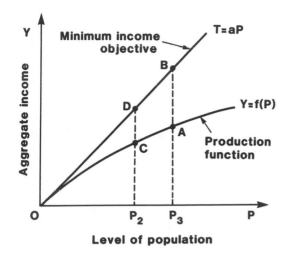

Figure 10.1 Ricardian case, in which the foreign-aid income support is only minimized when the population of the LDC is reduced to zero. In this case, the population of the LDC needs to be reduced to the minimum acceptable level in order to minimize the aid bill.

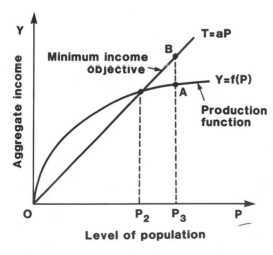

Figure 10.2 Ricardian case, in which all levels of population at or below a particular positive value in an LDC obviate the need for foreign aid to support income in the LDC.

MELLOR'S CASE:
CONSTANT RETURNS

Mellor's case is mentioned for the sake of completeness. Mellor considers a case in which constant returns to population size prevail and income is close to subsistence level so that there is no surplus for export (Mellor, 1985). Sufficient land is available for clearing and settlement to accommodate an increased population at a similar per capita income to that already available. Mellor suggests that this may have been typical of parts of Southeast Asia in the past.

In this case, the production function takes the linear form

$$Y = kP \tag{5}$$

where k is the average and marginal product of the population. If the target level of per capita income exceeds k, there is no level of population for which the target can be achieved by the country. In this case, where $a > k$, a zero population level minimizes the donor's aid bill, and the total falls as population falls. Thus it will be optimal from the donor's viewpoint to reduce P to P^*, as in the Ricardian situation illustrated by Figure 10.1. However, in this case the per capita subsidy remains constant as P falls, whereas it actually falls in the Ricardian situation illustrated by Figure 10.1. Of course, if $k \geqslant a$, no foreign aid is required.

THE MARSHALLIAN CASE:
INCREASING THEN DECREASING RETURNS

Marshall emphasized that at low levels of production and population increasing returns to scale are likely to prevail but give way to decreasing returns at higher levels (Marshall, 1961). This indicates a production function of an elongated S-form. For some SINS the Marshallian case may be more realistic than those discussed earlier. It will tend to be so if exchange and specialization are important and some manufacturing activities are present.

The Marshallian case contains more possibilities in relation to achieving target income levels than the previous two cases. Four situations can be distinguished: (1) the production function crosses the target line once (from above); (2) the production function crosses the target line twice (once from below and once from above); (3) the production function touches the target income line so that this line is tangential to it; (4) the production function is below the income target line for all values of P. These possibilities are illustrated by Figures 10.3 to 10.6, respectively. Let us consider each situation in turn.

In the situation shown in Figure 10.3, a population size of P_2 or less ensures that the per capita income goal is met without the need for aid. Thus if population is P_3, aid of AB is needed to achieve the target income. But if population is reduced to P_2, aid is no longer required. Further reduction in population will raise per capita income above A. While per capita income at first rises as P is reduced, it falls in value at lower levels of P as P is further reduced. In the case shown, it declines if P is reduced below P_1. However, any value of $P \leqslant P_2$ enables the donor's income goal to be met.

In the situation shown in Figure 10.4, any population level in the range $P_0 \leqslant P \leqslant P_2$ enables the donor's goal to be satisfied, if the minimum population objective P^* is not binding. Income per capita for the SIN, however, is maximized when $P = P_1$. Both at low levels of population ($0 < P < P_0$) and high levels of population ($P > P_2$) the donor is required to provide aid to meet the target level of income. Therefore, in this case, while some migration may be in the donor's interest, excessive migration is not.

The case illustrated in Figure 10.5 is a special one. There is only one positive value of P, namely P_2, for which the donor's goal can be satisfied. As population moves in either direction away from this value, the amount of foreign aid needed to fill the income gap rises for all values of $P > P_2$ and at first for values of $P < P_2$.

In the case shown in Figure 10.6, there is no positive value of P for which the income target can be met from the production of the SIN. However, apart from the corner-point minimum for the foreign aid supplement, S, for $P = 0$, a local minimum occurs for $P = P_2$. The required level of foreign aid, S, as a function of P takes the form indicated by the curve in Figure 10.7. Should $P_0 < P^* < P_2$, P_2 is the optimal population from the donor's viewpoint. Once again the donor has an interest in avoiding both "low" and "very high" levels of population in the SIN.

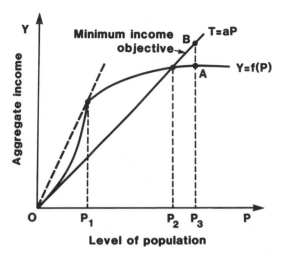

Figure 10.3 Marshallian case, in which all levels of population at or below a particular positive value in an LDC obviate the need for foreign aid to support income in the LDC.

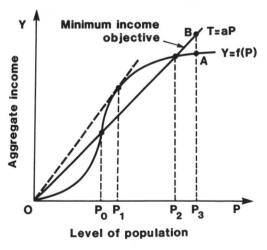

Figure 10.4 Marshallian case, in which levels of population only in a limited range or band below a particular positive population size in an LDC obviate the need for foreign aid to support income in the LDC.

144

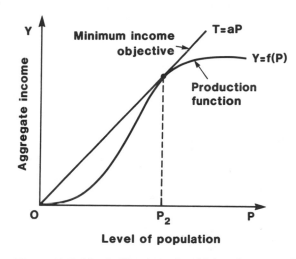

Figure 10.5 Marshallian case, in which only one positive level of population size in the LDC obviates the need for foreign aid to support incomes.

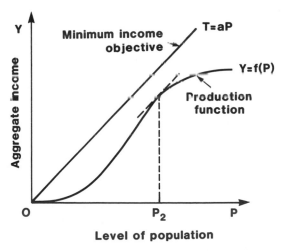

Figure 10.6 Marshallian case, in which no positive level of population size in the LDC obviates the need for foreign aid to support incomes.

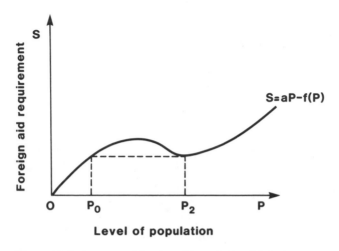

Figure 10.7 Amount of foreign aid needed to fill the income gap in an LDC in the Marshallian case where aid is needed whatever the (positive) level of population in the LDC.

Note also in Figure 10.6 that the level of population in the SIN that minimizes the donor's foreign aid bill is less than that which maximizes indigenous production per capita. This is a potential source of conflict between a SIN and a donor.

ALTERNATIVES TO POPULATION REDUCTION

Both capital accumulation and transfer of technology via aid can be considered as alternatives to income transfers and to population control. While some development practitioners are optimistic about the potential for capital accumulation and new or introduced technology to raise incomes in developing countries, the scope for this approach to development could be quite limited in many SINS in the Pacific given their meagre resource base. Possibly this is also Bertram's view (Bertram, 1986) in that he rejects the development of modern enterprises in micro-states in the Pacific as being culturally unacceptable and relatively unproductive. He says,

despite the high risks, high cost, and low probability of long-run "sustainability," this model of development [modernization model] continues to exercise considerable hold over the imagination of development planners in the Pacific area, especially those associated with major international aid organizations. The analysis of this paper suggests, however, that an externally-imposed "capitalist road" will prove a burdensome and expensive *cul-de-sac* for donors as well as islanders, and should not be pursued. [Bertram, 1986, p. 818]

It is a fallacy to believe that capital accumulation and new technology can raise or significantly raise the production of a country, no matter what is the availability and nature of its natural resources.

The natural resources of many SINS are extremely limited and offer litle prospect for productive investment (cf. Tisdell & I. J. Fairbairn, 1983, 1984; Bertram & Watters, 1985; Liew, 1986; Connell, 1986). Some atoll economies consist of little more than small limey outcrops ill-suited to agriculture, with no mineral resources of any consequence, and with the seas that surround them, while considered to be their most significant natural resource, not especially productive by world standards. Given the poverty of the natural resources available and the natural disadvantages encountered by many SINS such as remoteness from major markets, territorial fragmentation, and transport constraints, there appears to be little scope for productive foreign investment—that is, an investment that at least returns the original capital invested plus a surplus, however small. This is not to say that some productive investment may not be possible, but the scope is very limited. Hence, one cannot rely to any great extent on aid intended for productive investment and capital accumulation as a means for raising per capita income in SINS to target levels.

Apart from the obvious natural resource poverty of many SINS, in many of these countries other evidence points toward negative or low returns to investment on the whole. For example, Kiribati established an investment fund (Revenue Equalisation Reserve Fund) from royalties received for superphosphate mining on Banaba. This fund has been invested almost entirely abroad. The same is true of Nauru, which has a similar fund. An investment fund has also been established for Tuvalu in the form of a lump sum grant from Australia and the United Kingdom. This fund, which is managed by Westpac on behalf of the government of Tuvalu, will also be invested abroad. This seems to indicate that higher returns (probably much higher) on funds can be expected by investment outside these SINS than within them. Ex post facto evaluation of investment projects undertaken in many SINS also indicates negative or disappointing returns.

Prospects for productive investment in SINS thus appear to be very limited. Furthermore, where unproductive investment is undertaken with foreign aid, the loss in terms of opportunities foregone often exceeds that indicated by the monetary loss on the investment. This is because unproductive investment may draw local resources away from more productive uses and has a crowding-out effect. Of course, the social loss may be even greater if the investment dislocates the social and cultural pattern of the society or has adverse environmental or ecological consequences that are damaging to local production. Sometimes investment projects financed by foreign aid are grafted onto the social structure of developing countries rather than integrated into their structure at the grassroots level.

Donors may have a preference for aid for investment purposes rather than direct income transfers, and especially for aid that supports effort. This is a reflection of the puritanical belief in the Western world that reward should be for effort. Consequently, even investment aid involving a negative return may be preferred to "direct handouts." Aspects of the economic theory of the politics of bureaucracy and democracy may also reinforce bias in favor of capital accumulation.

Investment in projects within a country provides scope for beneficial economic gains or feedback to interests in the donor country. It may provide economic opportunities for consultants in the donor country (e.g., project evaluation) and for the sale of supplies and equipment. This helps to provide political support for the government aid bureaucracy from the interests involved (cf. Downs, 1957). As a rule there is also greater direct involvement of the donor in the aid-receiving country and more apparent dependence than in the case of mere income transfers, and this may appeal to some donors.

Turning now to the introduction of new technology, this also has optimistic supporters in donor countries as a means of achieving economic growth in developing countries. Much of this new technology is embodied in equipment. Similar reasons for donors favoring it apply as in the case of projects requiring capital investment: it provides a major role for the donor in the SIN, knowledge is asymmetric (the donor has more knowledge about the techniques to be transferred than the recipient), placing the recipient in a dependent position, and there is likely to be payoff or feedback to consultants and equipment suppliers in the donor country. However, the extent to which new technology and introduced technology is likely to be effective in raising incomes in a SIN is uncertain. While the introduction of some new technologies may increase productivity, no magical technology seems to be around the corner for substantially raising productivity in most SINS. Substantial reliance on the technology transfer strategy is likely to be ineffective in raising per capita income levels in SINS to target levels.

Some economists have argued that the transfer of technology from developed economies to less developed ones can be expected to inhibit the growth of the latter. Mandel (1975), for example, argues that technology transfer widens the market of the developed countries and is particularly to their advantage. Maitra (1980, 1986, 1988a) while being sympathetic to Mandel's viewpoint emphasizes the fact that such transfer can destroy existing indigenous technology and hinder its further development in less developed countries. However, they are disadvantaged from a long-term growth point of view. He says,

Because of negative impacts of technology and capital transfers, necessary reorganization of the economy to generate indigenous technology to make more productive utilisation of domestic resources has failed to take place. Consequently, problems of so-called overpopulation and income inequality have been and are being aggravated and, therefore, the gap between rich and poor—intranational and international—is widening as days go by. [Maitra, 1980, p. 89]

This is consistent with the view that contact of less developed countries with more developed ones gives rise to forces instrumental in bringing about de-development or fostering economic backwardness (Frank, 1978). In any case, technology transferred to less developed countries including SINS is not always appropriate for their factor composition, cultural/social situations, or environmental conditions. Many government aid agencies have a preference for long-term, big projects that can be managed by a company from the donor country rather than for supporting small projects arising out of grass roots needs and heavily reliant on indigenous technology and know-how (cf. Maitra, 1986, Ch. 2).

DISCUSSION

It has been suggested that there is little prospect of a number of resource-poor SINS in the Pacific being able to obtain self-sustaining economic growth and target levels of income through foreign aid intended for productive investment and technology transfer. Indeed, it is argued that the production function of many SINS may lie below the target level of aggregate income for them, and while it may be raised to a limited extent by investment and technology transfer, is unlikely to be moved above the target line by these means. This leaves these SINS with three other options to consider: (1) continuing to receive "disguised" income transfers through aid used for public service employment (or have some of it directed to informal sector promotion) and remaining dependent upon donors; (2) seeking emigration to the donor country; or (c) opting for autarky, with a much lower level of income but with greater preservation of traditional culture. None of these alternatives may appear particularly attractive to a SIN, but their choices are constrained by their resource-poor situation.

Bertram (1986) sees virtue in aid and income transfers being channeled more through informal sector promotion than is represented by government sector support. As he points out, this could have structural, political, social, and health advantages. He suggests that "planners might opt for the Pacific equivalent of an 'informal sector promoting' development process, with various types of subsidies channeled directly into the village economy" (ibid., p. 818). Of the alternatives, emigration may be the least unsatisfactory solution in terms of aid requirements. It *can* reduce dependence on donor nations and raise per capita income. On the other hand, it can accelerate changes in local culture and reduce productivity in the SIN. This is an option adopted by New Zealand for *some* SINS. However, not all donors are prepared to accept immigrants from SINS, even if this could reduce their foreign aid bill.

Australia, for example, has not extended special immigration status to people from any SIN. While the "White Australia" immigration policy no longer exists, all potential immigrants to Australia must compete for entry via the annual quota of immigrants on the basis of criteria such as professional or trade qualifications, demand for skills in Australia, and capital to be transferred to Australia. It is very difficult for islanders from the South Pacific to achieve entry, given these requirements. Furthermore, it is not clear that Australia would be prepared to grant special immigration status to inhabitants of any South Pacific SIN, even though this has been recommended by some groups (Ward, 1986). Australia has had a history of hostility to non-European immigrants that has only been modified in recent years. The origins of this hostility are complex, but it was based in the past on the perception of Australian trade unionists and workers that such immigrants would seriously compete with them for jobs. Furthermore, the history of Australia's involvement in using indentured labor ("Kanakas") from the South Pacific to work mainly in the sugar cane plantations of Queensland has probably meant that Australians have not been prepared to look at immigration from this part of the world in a detached manner (Ward, 1982, pp. 105–106). But this experience is now well in the past, and the time seems opportune to consider sympathetically the question of special status for immigrants from these areas, at least in relation to the very smallest nations such as Tuvalu and Kiribati. Their populations are so small that the effect of permitting immigration would be virtually imperceptible in Australia, but it could be of considerable benefit to these countries. Nevertheless, the opponents of such immigration may see it as the thin edge of the wedge leading on to extension to other larger countries.

Consideration must also be given to the question of whether a donor can be expected to aim to minimize the aid bill to a SIN subject to the condition of ensuring the inhabitants of the SIN a target level of income. To do this may reduce dependence on the donor and in some cases could lead to economic independence on the part of the SIN. For a number of reasons, a donor may wish to maintain the economic dependence of a SIN.

First, the SIN may be strategically important to the donor from a military or tactical point of view. Economic dependence places the donor in a strong position to influence the government of the SIN.

For example, it has been claimed that Palau (West Caroline Islands) is strategically important to the United States as a backup for bases for the Philippines. If bases should be lost in the Philippines, Palau can substitute. Clearly other islands in the mid-Pacific captured from Japan in World War II are also of strategic importance. Even if a SIN is not currently of strategic significance, situations can change, and some dependence may help the donor to keep *options* open in relation to international strategy.

Secondly, not all groups in the donor country have an interest in minimizing the country's foreign aid bill. In line with the theories of Downs (1957) and Niskanen (1971), government aid bodies such as AIDAB (Australian International Development Assistance Bureau) have an interest in expanding their aid activities, since this expands their bureaucracy. In this regard, they are supported by various "clients," such as companies and individuals in the donor country able to obtain economic contracts as a result of aid delivery.

Finally, as a result of dependence, the donor is given access to information about the recipient. Apart from the possible international strategic value of this, it can mean that the donor is first to know of any valuable commercial opportunity.

It might also be noted that residents of a donor country may not wish to see a SIN depopulated because they value the existence of its different culture and are prepared to give aid to support it. The culture and the community may have some existence value, in a way that is not dissimilar to the *existence* value of species of wildlife, even though it may appear to be poor taste to connect these two aspects (Walsh, Loomis, & Gillman, 1984).

CONCLUDING COMMENTS

The economic difficulties facing underdeveloped ministates in the Pacific are considerable. No ideal solution to their economic poverty appears to exist. However, for some ministates that do not currently have this option, the possibility of emigration to aid-donor countries is worth considering.[5] It can increase per capita income in a SIN and reduce the size of the aid required from the donor. Nevertheless, the relationship between emigration, per capita income in the SIN, and the required size of aid funds need not be a straightforward one, as consideration of alternative possible production relationships indicates. In particular if a Marshallian-type production relationship applies, there are limits on the extent to which population reduction can be used to increase income per head in a ministate. While there is no a priori reason to be pessimistic about emigration, it may not on its own be sufficient to raise per capita income in a SIN to an acceptable target level and can in some circumstances, if pressed too far, actually reduce per capita income. Clearly some empirical evidence is needed to determine the actual relationship between emigration and the level of per capita income in particular microstates.

Bertram (1986) argues that microeconomies in the Pacific should try to sustain aid and maintain their rent entitlements in terms of aid, philately, and migrant remittances. To do so is to forego self-reliance, to seek dependence, and to remain dependent. However, some microstates may be able to become more self-reliant by having migration outlets (or easier outlets) to certain developed countries. In addition, if a greater proportion of aid was to be used for village or informal sector promotion, as suggested by Bertram (1986) and Connell (1986) and implicit in Tisdell and I. J. Fairbairn (1984), healthier economic and social conditions could result. While Bertram (1986) claims that Tisdell and I. J. Fairbairn (1984) advocate the involution of these economies to subsistence, this is not really so. Rather, they were emphasizing in their model that international trade—and especially specialization for such trade—would involve major risks for these economies and that they might therefore wish to minimize dependence on such trade, even to the extent of increasing their subsistence activity levels. In any case, it is possible to agree with Bertram that a combination of expansion of productive activity and of international trade is unlikely to lead to sustainable development and adequate living standards in these countries, and one must, therefore, look to other strategies such as those discussed in this chapter (cf. de Vries, 1977).

NOTES

1. Bertram (1986) suggests that New Zealand tries to keep the per capita income of SINS most dependent on it in a fixed proportion to its own.

2. It is not being suggested that per capita income is an entirely satisfactory measure of welfare, and obviously income is difficult to measure

precisely. But some working assumptions are needed to make progress in discussing issues.

3. It also assumes that population change is an independent variable.

4. It is being assumed that emigrants will add to total production in the donor country and not merely replace indigenes in employment. If they are unemployed in the donor country or significantly so or cause unemployment of indigenes, the donor would need to take this into account, because although the foreign aid bill of the donor might go down as a result of emigration from a SIN, its social service payment bill could go up. This matter requires further investigation.

5. But before this policy is adopted, the donor needs to give consideration to whether the emigrants from the SIN concerned will add significantly to production in the donor country. If such migration would lead to increased social service payments in the donor country, this will need to be counterbalanced against any saving in foreign aid as a result of migration from the SIN. Although the matter appears complex, New Zealand's experience with migrants from SINS may give an indication of effects in the donor country. Some empirical work in relation to this matter is possible. It might also be mentioned that some nations favor temporary to permanent migration. But this can be especially damaging to productivity and the social structure in a SIN.

11

Concluding Assessment of Resource Issues

Rational choice about resource-use requires knowledge of what is technically or scientifically possible and what is desired or wanted. Considerable uncertainty exists about the ability of natural resources in particular to support in perpetuity a growing level of economic production and about our ability to avoid serious environmental deterioration as a result of rising resource use. This is partially because the rate of future technological and scientific progress is unknown and because there are differences of opinion between natural scientists about trends in global environmental conditions and about the imminence of possible major global environmental change resulting from the effects of economic activity. But today it is more commonly accepted that there may be environmental and resource limits both to the speed of economic growth and the length of time for which a high rate of economic growth can be maintained, and that these limits can be expected to become increasingly relevant to public policy. In the last few years, supply-side and waste-side limitations, rather than demand-side factors, have been increasingly seen by some economists and the public at large as important considerations in the assessment of the desirability of economic growth and development and as being of

importance for public policy. Public policy in this area is complicated by uncertainty both on the technical side as well as on the
evaluation side.

UNCERTAINTY

Not only is there uncertainty about future production possibilities and the environmental consequences of increasing
economic activity, but there is conflict about appropriate values and
uncertainty about what is desired or likely to be desired in the
future. Apart from the income distributional conflict between individuals currently alive, environmental examples of which have been
given in earlier chapters, collective choice is complicated by conflicts between individuals over values and by the types of risk and
uncertainty mentioned.

The values of individuals can be in sharp conflict. Some, for
instance, espouse man-centered ethics, whereas others may
espouse a more naturalistic philosophy. Some believe that considerable regard should be paid to the possible welfare of future
generations, whereas others may believe that little attention should
be given to this. There is often no easy way to settle such conflict.

Collective risk and uncertainty also make it more difficult to
select optimal economic growth and environmental policies,
because different individuals often have quite different attitudes to
the bearing of risk and uncertainty to which they are collectively
exposed. Some may be extremely risk-averse, whereas others may
be more inclined to gamble, in relation to possible consequences
both for themselves and for future generations.

Long-term planning is also made more difficult because the
preferences of future generations can at best only be imperfectly
predicted, and future levels of the world's population cannot be
predicted with accuracy. Given such uncertainty as well as uncertainty on the supply-side, it has been argued that it is a wise policy to
err on the side of conserving natural resources, thereby maintaining
flexibility and keeping options open for resource-use.

But not everyone accepts the proposition that this is the best way
to assist future generations or even ourselves in relation to future
possibilities. Tietenberg (1988) suggests that in some circumstances
it may be preferable to deplete resources and to use the income to

finance a greater amount of research and development, which could then assist future generations through greater technological progress and the availability of more knowledge than otherwise. Certainly, to argue that in view of our situation one might err optimally on the side of conservation is not to suggest that an unlimited amount of conservation is optimal.

IMPORTANT QUESTIONS

This book has been concerned with questions of economic scarcity, particularly between generations, over time, and between developed and less developed nations. In particular, it has been concerned about whether economic growth and environmental changes will impoverish us in the future, impoverish future generations, or create an economic catastrophe as a result of natural resource depletion and pollution. In relation to less developed nations, some of the issues discussed are their prospects of achieving sustained economic growth and maintaining it, conservation of natural resources by them and their economic welfare, the role of urban–rural migration and industrialization in reducing their economic poverty, and the value of international migration and income transfers (compared to foreign technical aid and capital aid) as a means of effectively assisting the population of those less developed nations that have an extremely restricted natural resource base and, in general, suffer from inherent resource-poverty. Some small island nations in the Pacific and the Caribbean seem to fall into this category.

It might be noted that, especially in the 1970s, the slogan "trade, not aid" was widely acclaimed as suggesting an effective means on the part of developed nations to assist less developed ones. The argument in favor of this was often combined with the view that foreign aid retards development in less developed countries. But, as suggested in this book, neither trade nor aid can provide a way out of poverty for the residents of some resource-poor nations, and their best prospects for economic improvement may lie in being able to participate in international migration to more developed countries. This may particularly be the case for island ministates such as those in the Pacific and the Caribbean. This is not to say that

migrants from such areas are always welcomed in developed countries.

POPULATION POLICY

Economics, especially as it has evolved in the Western world,
relies strongly on anthropocentric values. Not only does humanity
appear to be the measure of all things including policies, but it is the
purpose of them. Even those suggested value systems that would
subordinate the desires or wants of individuals to "higher" values,
still tend to be human-centered. This is, for example, true of the
view of Georgescu-Roegen (1975) and of Daly (1980) that the
fundamental aim of human policy should be to ensure that the
human species survives for as long as possible. For instance, Daly
proposes that the utilitarian principle of the "greatest good for the
greatest number" be replaced by the following: (1) the longest
possible period of existence for the human species; and (2) the
presence during this period of the greatest number of people possible at a satisfactory minimum level of income or consumption.
Thus his proposals seem to accord with a recent car bumper-sticker:
"Live simply that others may simply live," if we assume that "the
others" are restricted to human beings.

This emphasizes that long-term resource alternatives cannot be
assessed independently of optimal population issues, and of our
values in relation to human populations' patterns and sizes. While it
is not appropriate to launch into this matter in depth at this stage,
some of the main choices confronting us about human population
can be seen from Figure 11.1. Assume that the human species will
remain in existence for only one more period (length undefined).
Income per capita as a function of population during this period is
assumed to increase at low levels of population as population is
raised and then decline so that an inverted U-shaped curve as shown
by ABC in Figure 11.1 applies. Suppose also that a minimum
satisfactory level per capita income for survival is equal to OD.

Income per head is at a maximum in the survival period when a
population of P_2 is achieved. But this does not maximize the sum of
utility for society, because if each individual obtains approximately
equal utility from income and this increases at a decreasing rate as

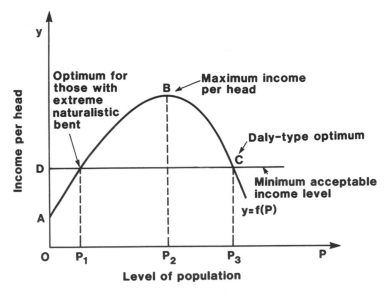

Figure 11.1 Different optimal levels of human population in relation to income per head.

income rises, a population greater than P_2 will maximize the *sum* of utility. Application of the utilitarian principle will result in a population greater than that which maximizes income per head but *usually* smaller than the population selected as optimal by Daly's principle. In the case illustrated in Figure 11.1, Daly's principle indicates that a population level of P_3 is optimal.

From Figure 11.2 it can be seen that a population that maximizes total utility for society is generally greater than that which maximizes utility per head or income per head if utility per head rises with per capita income at a decreasing rate. Let the curve HJK represent the utility obtained by each individual as a function of the level of population. This curve reaches a maximum at J for a population level of P_2. The total utility obtained by society at point J is the same anywhere along the rectangular hyperbole indicated by W_1W_1. Clearly a population higher than P_2 will enable a higher iso-utility line for society to be reached. For example, the level of collective utility corresponding to the rectangular hyperbole W_2W_2

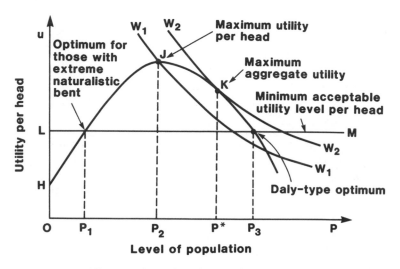

Figure 11.2 Differences in optimal levels of human population in relation to utility per head for different types of valuation.

could be reached for a population level P^*. In fact, point K corresponds to the optimum from a utilitarian point of view. This may be closer to Daly's ideal than the population level that maximizes income per head, namely P_2.

Both the utilitarian principle and Daly's doctrine will, of course, be rejected by individuals who hold that living things other than humans have a right to existence. Indeed, it is conceivable that some with a strong naturalistic bent might advocate a policy at the opposite end of the spectrum to Daly's. If a greater human population always tends to be at the expense of other species, some advocates of nature conservation may argue that the optimal policy is to aim for the smallest possible human population consistent with continuance of the human species subject to a minimum acceptable level of per capita income being obtained. This would imply a population level of P_1 in the case illustrated in Figures 11.1 and 11.2. While not all holders of naturalistic ethics take such an extreme position, the general implication of such ethics is that it is desirable to restrain human population in the interest of saving other species and their populations.

DISTRIBUTIONAL JUSTICE WITHIN AND
BETWEEN GENERATIONS

But leaving the matter of the relevance of naturalistic ethics to one side for the time being, another controversial subject is how to determine the ideal distribution of income both between individuals within generations and between generations. While it is not possible here to explore all the issues involved, some points are worth considering. Rawls' principle is increasingly advocated as a basis for settling conflict between generations over the distribution of income. It implies that the distribution of income between individuals should be equal, unless inequality is to the benefit of all (Rawls, 1971). Equality is claimed to be just, since any of us could have been born into the situation of any other person. If we were to go behind the "veil of ignorance," not knowing what situation we would be born into, then we would settle for an equal distribution of income, according to Rawls' principle.

It is sometimes argued on this principle that the income per head of future generations should therefore be at the same level as it is at present (Tietenberg, 1988, pp. 32–33, p. 492). But our income is higher than that of earlier generations. Is that just? It could be, according to Rawls' principle, if this has occurred because of actions taken by previous generations which benefited them but indirectly benefited us—that is, actions that were to the benefit of all.

In assessing Rawls' principle, there are many aspects that we need to consider. Could we, in fact, equally as well have been born into the position of any other and at any other time? It is not clear that this is so. But if one accepts that it is so, then one can ask the further question of whether one could equally as well have been born as *any* living thing. If so, does this imply that the Rawlsian principle should be extended completely or partially to all living things?

In addition, how far do we extend Rawls' principles in relation to man? It is not just a matter of considering the distribution of income, but questions arise about the right to be conceived and to live. Population levels become a policy variable. It could be argued that our conception is a chance phenomenon and so, therefore, is the fact that we live as individuals at all. Assuming that all would want to live who have *a chance* to do so, this seems to support Daly's principle of ensuring that the maximum number of individuals live at a minimum acceptable level. This, however, brings us full circle in the argument, for it naturally raises again the question of what are the rights to existence of other living things.

Answers to such questions depend very much on one's view of the cosmos as well as on one's ethics. Those who believe in the possibility of reincarnation and the possibility of being reborn in other than human form, as do the Hindus, may have an entirely different view of these matters including optimal population policies to Christians with their belief in the prospect of Heaven, to Jews or to Muslims, to atheists or to agnostics. Thus we are eventually driven back to basic philosophy or philosophies in our attempt to grapple with resource issues. We need to keep this firmly in mind because all of our economic modeling and our policy prescriptions are based upon general philosophical preconceptions. It is all too easy to ignore this. Economics and philosophy are inextricably linked. The main danger occurs when economists fail to realize the nexus or make it explicit. It is especially dangerous to ignore this nexus when discussing questions of long-term economic development, like many of those which have been raised in this book.

CONCLUDING COMMENTS

All the topics covered in this book have been concerned with dynamic and changing aspects of our existence. This is equally true of the discussion concerning the use of natural resources, the conservation of living things and their environments, biological control of pests, migration and human settlements, the position of less developed countries in relation to more developed ones, and income distribution issues. To the extent that static analysis has been used, this has only been done for illustrative purposes. We are concerned essentially with a world of continual change. Indeed, it may be impossible for human beings (during human existence) ever to reach a stationary state in relation to the environment, even though we are always moving toward it (Georgescu-Roegen, 1971). However, we can clearly choose development paths that involve less variation and may be sustainable for longer than our present path. This book has emphasized that in the choice of a suitable development path, we cannot be safely guided by individualistic self-interest alone but must pay attention to relationships between human beings *and* between humans and Nature. Philosophy, economics, and ecology all have a role to play in determining how best the human race can use scarce resources, especially scarce natural resources, as it charts its uncertain path through time.

References and Bibliography

Alauddin, M., and Tisdell, C. (1986). "Market analysis, technological change and income distribution in semi-subsistence agriculture: The case of Bangladesh." *Agricultural Economics*, 1: 1–18.

Alauddin, M., and Tisdell, C. (1988a). "Has the 'green revolution' destabilized food production? Some evidence from Bangladesh." *The Developing Economies*, 26 (2): 142–60.

Alauddin, M., and Tisdell, C. (1988b). "New agricultural technology and sustainable food production: Bangladesh's achievements, predicament and prospects." in C. Tisdell and P. Maitra (Eds.), *Technological Change, Development and the Environment: Socio-Economic Perspectives* (pp. 35–62). London: Routledge.

Alauddin, M., and Tisdell, C. (1988c). "Impact of new agricultural technology on the instability of foodgrain production and yield: Data analysis for Bangladesh and its districts." *Journal of Development Economics*, 29: 199–227.

Alauddin, M., and Tisdell, C. (1989). "Rural poverty and resource distribution in Bangladesh: 'Green revolution' and beyond." In B. Greenshields and M. Bellamy (Eds.), *Government Intervention in Agriculture: Cause and Effect* (pp. 247–253). Aldershot, Hants, U.K.: Dartmouth Publishing.

Arrow, K. J., and Fisher, A. C. (1974). "Environmental preservation, uncertainty and irreversibility." *Quarterly Journal of Economics*, 88: 313–319.

Auld, B. A., Menz, K. M., and Tisdell, C. A. (1987). *Weed Control Economics*. London: Academic Press.

Barber, W. J. (1961). *The Economy of British Central Africa*. Stanford, CA: Stanford University Press.

Barbier, E. B. (1987). "The concept of sustainable economic development." *Environmental Conservation*, 14 (2): 101–110.

Barnett, H. J., and Morse, C. (1963). *Scarcity and Growth*. Baltimore, MD: Johns Hopkins University Press.

Basu, K. (1984). *The Less Developed Economy: A Critique of Contemporary Theory*. Oxford, U.K.: Basil Blackwell.

Baumol, W. J., and Oates, W. E. (1979). *Economics, Environmental Policy and the Quality of Life*. Englewood Cliffs, NJ: Prentice Hall.

Baumol, W. J., and Quandt, R. (1964). "Rules of thumb and optimally imperfect decisions." *American Economic Review*, 54: 23–64.

Berle, A. A., and Means, G. C. (1932). *The Modern Corporation and Private Property*. New York: Macmillan.

Bertram, I. G. (1986). "Sustainable development in Pacific microeconomies." *World Development*, 14 (7): 809–992.

Bertram, I. G., and Watters, R. F. (1985). "The MIRAB economy in South Pacific microstates." *Pacific Viewpoint*, 26 (3): 497–519.

Bertram, I. G., and Watters, R. F. (1986). "The MIRAB process: Some earlier analysis in context." *Pacific Viewpoint*, 27 (1): 47–59.

Bishop, R. C. (1978). "Endangered species and uncertainty: The economics of a safe minimum standard." *American Journal of Agricultural Economics*, 60 (1): 10–18.

Bishop, R. C. (1979). "Endangered species, irreversibility and uncertainty: A reply." *American Journal of Agricultural Economics*, 61 (2): 377–379.

Blainey, G. (1976). *Triumph of the Nomads: A History of Ancient Australia*. South Melbourne, Victoria, Australia: Sun Books.

Boulding, K. E. (1966). "The Economics of the Coming Spaceship Earth." in H. Jarrett (Ed.), *Environmental Quality in a Growing Economy* (pp. 3–14). Baltimore, MD: Johns Hopkins Press.

Brown, C. V., and Jackson, P. M. (1986). *Public Sector Economics*, 3rd ed. Oxford, U.K.: Basil Blackwell.

Caldecott, J., and Nyaoi, A. (1985). *Hunting in Sarawak*. National Parks and Wildlife Office, Sarawak Forest Department, Jalan Gartak, Kuching.

Chaudhri, D. P., and Dasgupta, A. K. (1985). *Agriculture and the Development Process*. London: Croom Helm.

Chisholm, A. H. (1988). "Sustainable resource use and development: Uncertainty, irreversibility and rational choice." In C. Tisdell and

P. Maitra (Eds.), *Technological Change, Development and the Environment: Socio-Economic Perspectives* (pp. 188–216). London: Routledge.

Ciriacy-Wantrup, S.V. (1968). *Resource Conservation: Economics and Policies*, 3rd ed. Berkeley, CA: University of California, Division of Agricultural Science.

Clark, C. W. (1976). *Mathematical Bioeconomics*. New York: John Wiley.

Clark, W. C., and Munn, R. E. (1986). *Sustainable Development of the Biosphere*. Cambridge, U.K.: Cambridge University Press.

Clarke, W. C. (1971). *Place and People: An Ecology of a New Guinea Community*. Canberra, Australia: Australian National University Press.

Clawson, M. (1959). *Methods of Measuring Demand for and Value of Outdoor Recreation*, RFF reprint No. 10. Washington, D.C.: Resources for the Future.

Clawson, M., and Knetsch, J. L. (1966). *Economics of Outdoor Recreation*. Baltimore, MD: Johns Hopkins Press.

Common, M. S., and Pearce, D. W. (1973). "Adaptive mechanisms, growth and the environment: The case of natural resources." *Canadian Journal of Economics*, 6: 289–300.

Connell, J. (1986). "Population, migration and problems of atoll development in the South Pacific." *Pacific Studies*, 9 (2): 41–55.

Conway, G. R. (1985). "Agroecosystem analysis." *Agricultural Administration*, 20: 31–55.

Conway, G. R. (1987). "The properties of agroecosystems." *Agricultural Systems*, 24: 95–117.

Daly, H. (1980). *Economics, Ecology and Ethics*. San Francisco, CA: Freeman.

Darby, J. T. (1987). "Aspects of the conservation of the Yellow-eyed Penguin, habitat rehabilitation and planting strategies." Dunedin, South Island, N.Z.: Otago Museum, mimeo.

Day, D. (1981). *The Doomsday Book of Animals*. London: Edbury Press.

de Vries, B. A. (1977). "Development aid to small countries." In P. Selwyn (Ed.), *Development Policy in Small Countries* (pp. 164–184). London: Croom Helm.

DeBach, A. (1974). *Biological Control by Natural Enemies*. Cambridge, U.K.: Cambridge University Press.

Douglass, G. K. (1984). "The meanings of agricultural sustainability." In G. K. Douglass (Ed.), *Agricultural Sustainability in a Changing World Order* (pp. 3–29). Boulder, CO: Westview Press.

Downs, A. (1957). *An Economic Theory of Democracy*. New York: Harper & Row.

168 References and Bibliography

Edwards, G. W., and Freebairn, J. W. (1982). "The social benefits from an increase in production in part of an industry." *Review of Marketing and Agricultural Economics*, 50: 193–210.

Ehrlich, P. R. (1970). *The Population Bomb*. New York: Ballatine Books.

Ehrlich, P. R., Ehrlich, A. H., and Holdren, J. P. (1976). *Ecoscience: Population, Resources and Development*, 3rd ed. San Francisco, CA: Freeman.

Ehrlich, P. R., and Harriman, L. (1971). *How to Be a Survivor*. New York: Ballantine Books.

Ekins, P. (1986). *The Living Economy: A New Economics in the Making*. London: Routledge and Kegan Paul.

Fairbairn, T. I. J. (1985). *Island Economies: Studies from the South Pacific*. Suva, Fiji: Institute of Pacific Studies, University of South Pacific.

Fei, J. C., and Ranis, G. (1964). *Development of the Labour Surplus Economy: Theory and Policy*. Homewood, IL: Irwin.

Fisher, I. (1930). *The Nature of Capital and Incomes*. New York: Macmillan.

Forrester, J. W. (1971). *World Dynamics*. Cambridge, MA: Wright-Allen.

Frank, A. G. (1978). *Dependent Accumulation and Underdevelopment*. London: Macmillan.

Georgescu-Roegen, N. (1971). *The Entropy Law and the Economic Process*. Cambridge, MA: Harvard University Press.

Georgescu-Roegen, N. (1975). "Energy and economic myths." *Southern Economic Journal*, 40: 347–381.

Georgescu-Roegen, N. (1976). *Energy and Economic Myths: Institutional and Analytical Economic Essays*. New York: Pergamon Press.

Gordon, H. S. (1954). "The economic theory of a common property resource: The fishery." *Journal of Political Economy*, 62: 124–144.

Griliches, Z. (1957). "Hybrid corn: An exploration in the economics of agricultural research." *Econometrica*, 25: 501–522.

Harrod, R. F. (1939). "An essay in dynamic theory." *Economic Journal*, 59: 14–33.

Harrod, R. F. (1948). *Towards a Dynamic Economics*. London: Macmillan.

Hart, A. G. (1942). "Risk, uncertainty and the unprofitability of compounding probabilities." In O. Lange, F. McIntyre, and F. Yntema (Eds.), *Studies in Mathematical Economics and Econometrics* (pp. 110–118). Chicago, IL: The University of Chicago Press.

Harting, J. E. (1880). *British Animals Extinct in Historic Times*. London: Trubner.

Hartley, K., and Tisdell, C. A. (1981). *Micro-Economic Policy*. Chichester, Sussex, U.K.: Wiley.

Hayami, Y., and Herdt, R. W. (1975). "Market price effects of technological change on income distribution in semi-subsistence agriculture."
American Journal of Agricultural Economics, 59: 245–256.

Hazell, B. R. (1986). "Introduction." In B. Hazell (Ed.), *Summary Proceedings of a Workshop Cereal Yield Variability*. Washington, DC:
International Food Policy Research Institute.

Headley, J. C. (1985). "Cost–benefit analysis: Defining research needs." In
M. A. Hoy and D. C. Herzog (Eds.), *Biological Control in Agri-
cultural IPM Systems* (pp. 347–372). Orlando, FL: Academic
Press.

Hicks, J. R. (1949). "Mr Harrod's dynamic theory." *Economica*, 16: 106–
121.

Hirshleifer, J. (1976). *Price Theory and Applications*. Englewood Cliffs,
NJ: Prentice Hall.

Hoogvelt, A. M. M. (1978). *The Sociology of Developing Societies*, 2nd ed.
London: Macmillan.

Huffaker, C. B., and Caltagirone, L. E. (1986). "The impact of biological
control on the development of the Pacific." *Agriculture, Ecosystems and the Environment*, 15: 95–107.

Huffaker, C. B., Simmonds, F. J., and Laing, J. E. (1976). "The theoretical
and empirical basis of biological control." In C. B. Huffaker and P.
S. Messenger (Eds.), *Theory and Practice of Biological Control*
(pp. 41–71). New York: Academic Press.

Industries Assistance Commission (1985). *Report on the Biological Control
of Echium Species (Including Paterson's Curve/Salvation Jane)*.
Canberra, Australia: Australian Government Publishing Service.

IUCN (1980). *World Conservation Strategy*. Glands, Switzerland: International Union for the Conservation of Nature and Natural
Resources.

Jefferies, B. E. (1982). "Sagarmatha National Park: The impact of tourism
on the Himalayas." *Ambio*, 11 (5): 246–251.

Jevons, W. S. (1906). *The Coal Question*, 3rd ed. London: Macmillan.

Johannes, R. E. (1981). *Words of the Lagoon: Fishing and Marine Law in
the Palau District of Micronesia*. Berkeley, CA: University of
California Press.

Joint Committee on Foreign Affairs, Defence and Trade, The Parliament
of the Commonwealth of Australia (1989). *Australia's Relations
with the South Pacific*. Canberra, Australia: Australian Government Publishing Service.

Jones, H. G. (1975). *An Introduction to Modern Theories of Economic
Growth*. London: Nelson.

Jorgenson, D. W. (1967). "Surplus agricultural labour and the development of a dual economy." *Oxford Economic Papers*, 19: 288–312.

Julien, M. H., Kern, J. D., and Chan, R. R. (1984). "Biological control of weeds: An evaluation." *Protection Ecology*, 7: 3–25.

Kahn, H., Brown, W., and Martel, L. (1976). *The Next 200 Years: A Scenario for America and the World*. New York: William Morrow.

Kelley, A. C., Williamson, J. G., and Cheetham, R. J. (1972). *Dualistic Economic Development: Theory and History*. Chicago, IL: University of Chicago Press.

Kindleberger, C. P. (1965). *Economic Development*, 2nd ed. New York: McGraw-Hill.

Klee, G. A. (1980). *World Systems of Traditional Resource Management*. London: Edward Arnold.

Krutilla, J. V. (1967). "Conservation reconsidered." *American Economic Review*, 57: 777–786.

Kuznets, S. (1963). "Quantitative aspects of economic growth of nations: Distribution of income by size." *Economic Development and Cultural Change*, 11 (2): 1–80.

Lecomber, R. (1979). *The Economics of Natural Resources*. London: Macmillan.

Leibenstein, H. (1957). *Economic Backwardness and Economic Growth: Studies in the Theory of Economic Development*. New York: Wiley.

Leopold, A. (1933). *Game Management*. New York: Scribner.

Leopold, A. (1966). *A Sand Country Almanac: With Other Essays from Round River*. New York: Oxford University Press.

Lewis, W. A. (1954). "Economic development with unlimited supplies of labour." *The Manchester School*, 22: 139–191.

Lewis, W. A. (1965). *The Theory of Economic Growth*. London: George Allen and Unwin.

Lewis, W. A. (1979). "The dual economy revisited." *The Manchester School of Economic and Social Studies*, 47 (3): 211–229.

Liew, J. (1986). "Sustainable development and environmental management of atolls." *Occasional Paper No. 1*. The Integrated Atoll Development Project. Suva, Fiji: UNDP.

Little, I. M. D. (1982). *Economic Development*. Oxford, U.K.: Basil Blackwell.

Little, I. M. D., and Mirrlees, J. A. (1974). *Project Appraisal and Planning for Developing Countries*. London: Heinemann.

Maitra, P. (1980). *The Mainspring of Economic Development*. London: Croom Helm.

Maitra, P. (1986). *Population, Technology and Development*. Aldershot, U.K.: Gower.

Maitra, P. (1988a). "Population, technology and development: The India case with a critique of Marxists interpretations." In C. A. Tisdell and P. Maitra (Eds.), *Technological Change, Development and the Environment: Socio-Economic Perspectives* (pp. 9–34). London and New York: Routledge.

Maitra, P. (1988b). "Energy resources, technological change and economic dependence." In *Proceedings of Asian and Pacific Conference on Energy and Economic Development* (pp. 197–214). Taibei, Taiwan: International Association for Energy Economics.

Maitra, P. (1988c). "Technological change and the question of linkages between agriculture and industry—Case studies of Japan and India." *Economic Discussion Papers* No. 88/08. University of Otago, P.O. Box 56, Dunedin, South Island, New Zealand. Paper presented at the 8th International Economic Association Congress, New Delhi.

Malthus, T. R. (1798). *An Essay on the Principle of Population as It Affects the Future Improvement of Mankind*. London: J. Johnson.

Mandel, E. (1975). *Late Capitalism*. London: New Left Books.

Mao, Y. (1988). "The distribution of movement of U.S. population and regional economic development—A comment on 'Regional diversity: Growth in the U.S.'." *American Studies*, 1:67–83 (in Chinese).

Marris, R. (1964). *The Economic Theory of Managerial Capitalism*. London: Macmillan.

Marshall, A. (1961). *Principles of Economics*, 9th (variorum) edition. London: Macmillan.

McArthur, A. T. G. (1987). "Economic weights for breeding objectives." Lincoln College, N.Z., mimeo. A paper presented at the Australian Agricultural Economics Conference, Blenheim, New Zealand.

McKee, D., and Tisdell, C. (1988). "Development implications of migration from and between small island nations." *International Migration*, 26: 417–426.

McKee, D., and Tisdell, C. (forthcoming). *Development Issues in Small Island Economies*. New York: Praeger.

Meadows, D. L., Randers, J., and Beherens, W. (1972). *The Limits of Growth: A Report for the Club of Rome's Projection on the Predicament of Mankind*. New York: Universe Books.

Meier, G. M. (1964). *Leading Issues in Economic Development*. New York: Oxford University Press.

Meier, G. M. (1976). *Leading Issues in Economic Development*, 3rd ed. New York: Oxford University Press.

Mellor, J. W. (1985). "Determinants of rural poverty: The dynamics of production and prices." In J. W. Mellor and G. M. Desai (Eds.),

Agricultural Change and Rural Poverty: Variations on a Theme by Dharm Narian (pp. 21–40). Baltimore, MD: Johns Hopkins.

Mellor, J. W., and Desai, G. M. (1985). *Agricultural Change and Rural Poverty: Variations on a Theme by Dharm Narian*. Baltimore, MD: Johns Hopkins.

Mentis, M. T. (1964). "White Paper on agricultural policy." *South African Journal of Science*, 80: 538.

Mishan, E. J. (1967). *The Costs of Economic Growth*. London: Staples Press.

Mishra, H. R. (1982). "Balancing human needs and conservation in Nepal's Royal Chitwan National Park." *Ambio*, 11 (5): 246–251.

Nickum, J., and Dixon, J. (1989). "Environmental problems and modernisation." In C. E. Morrison and R. F. Dernberger, *Asia-Pacific Report, 1989. Focus: China in the Reform Era* (pp. 83–91). Honolulu, HI: East–West Center.

Niskanen, W. (1971). *Bureaucracy and Representative Government*. Chicago, IL: Aldine.

Nordhaus, W. (1974). "Resources as a constraint on economic growth." *American Economic Review, Papers and Proceedings*, 41–44.

Nordhaus, W. D., and Tobin, J. (1972). "Is growth obsolete?" In National Bureau of Economic Research, *Economic Growth*. New York: Columbia University Press.

Passmore, J. A. (1974). *Man's Responsibility for Nature—Ecological Problems and Western Traditions*. London: Duckworth.

Penrose, E. (1959). *The Theory of the Growth of the Firm*. Oxford, U.K.: Basil Blackwell.

Pigou, A. C. (1932). *Economics of Welfare*, 3rd ed. London: Macmillan.

Plucknett, D. L., Smith, N. J., Williams, J. T., and Anishetty, N. M. (1986). *Gene Banks and the World's Food*. Princeton, N.J.: Princeton University Press.

Podder, N. (1988). "Technology and its transfer to less developed economies." In C. Tisdell and P. Maitra (Eds.), *Technological Change, Development and the Environment: Socio-Economic Perspectives* (pp. 63–91). London: Routledge.

Randall, A. (1986). "Human preferences, economics and the conservation of species." In B. G. Norton (Ed.), *The Preservation of Species: The Value of Biological Diversity* (pp. 79–109). Princeton, NJ: Princeton University Press.

Ranis, G., and Fei, J. C. (1961). "A theory of economic development." *The American Economic Review*, 5: 533–565.

Rawls, J. (1971). *A Theory of Justice*. Cambridge, MA: Harvard University Press.

Redclift, M. (1987). *Sustainable Development: Exploring the Contradictions*. London: Methuen.

Ricardo, D. (1817). *The Principles of Political Economy and Taxation*. London.

Richardson, H. W. (1978). *Regional and Urban Economics*. Harmondsworth, Middlesex: Penguin.

Robbins, L. (1932). *An Essay on the Nature and Significance of Economic Science*. London: Macmillan.

Robbins, L. (1937). *An Essay on the Nature and Significance of Economic Science*, 2nd ed. London: Macmillan.

Rostow, W. W. (1960). *The Stages of Economic Growth*. Cambridge, U.K.: Cambridge University Press.

Roy, P., and Connell, J. (1989). "The greenhouse effect. Where have all the islands gone?" *Pacific Island Monthly*, April/May: 16–27.

Rudge, M. R. (1986). "Presidential address: Science, land management and accountability." *New Zealand Journal of Ecology*, 9: 1–9.

Sathiendrakumar, R., and Tisdell, C. A. (1987). "Migration from traditional rural communities and outside employment: A study of Maldivian fishing villages." *South East Asian Economic Review*, 8 (2): 121–163

Scott, A. D. (1955). *Natural Resources and the Economics of Conservation*. Toronto, Canada: University of Toronto Press.

Simon, H. (1957). *Models of Man*. New York: Wiley.

Simon, H. (1961). *Administrative Behavior*, 2nd ed. New York: Macmillan Company.

Simon, J. (1977). *The Economics of Population Growth*. Princeton, NJ/London: Princeton University Press.

Sinha, S. (1984). "Growth of scientific temper: Rural context." In M. Gibbons, P. Gummett, and B. Udgaonkar (Eds.), *Science and Technology Policy in the 1980s and Beyond* (pp. 166–190). London: Longmans.

Slade, M.E. (1982). "Trends in natural resource commodity prices: An analysis of the time domain." *Journal of Environmental Economics and Management*, 9: 122–127.

Smith, V. K., and Krutilla, J. V. (1979). "Endangered species, irreversibilities, and uncertainty: A comment." *American Journal of Agricultural Economics*, 61: 371–375.

Solow, R. M. (1956). "A contribution to the theory of economic growth." *Quarterly Journal of Economics*, 70: 65–94.

Solow, R. M. (1957). "Technical change and the aggregate production function." *Review of Economics and Statistics*, 39: 312–320.

Stahel, C., and Gales, R. (1987). *Little Penguin: Fairy Penguin in*

Australia. Kensington, Australia: University of New South Wales Press.

Tietenberg, T. (1988). *Environmental and Natural Resource Economics*, 2nd ed. Glenview, IL: Scott, Foresman.

Tisdell, C. A. (1968). *The Theory of Price Uncertainty, Production and Profit*. Princeton, NJ: Princeton University Press.

Tisdell, C. A. (1970). "Implications of learning for economic planning." *Economics of Planning*, 10 (3): 172–192.

Tisdell, C. A. (1972). *Microeconomics: The Theory of Economic Allocation*. Sydney, Australia: Wiley.

Tisdell, C. A. (1975). "The theory of optimal city-sizes: Some elementary considerations." *Urban Studies*, 12: 61–70.

Tisdell, C. A. (1981). *Science and Technology Policy: Priorities of Governments*. London: Chapman and Hall.

Tisdell, C. A. (1982). *Microeconomics of Markets*. Brisbane, Australia: Wiley.

Tisdell, C. A. (1983a). "An economist's critique of the world conservation strategy with examples from Australian experience." *Environmental Conservation*, 10 (1): 43–52.

Tisdell, C. A. (1983b). "Conserving living resources in third world countries." *International Journal of Environmental Studies*, 22: 11–24.

Tisdell, C. A. (1983c). "Optimal choice of a variety of a species for variable environmental conditions." *Journal of Agricultural Economics*, 34: 172–185.

Tisdell, C. A. (1986). "Conflicts about living marine resources in Southeast Asian and Australian waters: Turtles and dugong as cases." *Marine Resource Economics*, 3 (1): 89–109.

Tisdell, C. A. (1987a). "Economic evaluation of biological weed control." *Plant Protection Quarterly*, 2 (1): 10–12.

Tisdell, C. A. (1987b). "Particular economic problems faced by microstates in the South Pacific, especially atoll-based countries, and Australian policies." Sub-Committee on the South Pacific, Parliamentary Joint Committee on Foreign Affairs and Defence, *Hansard*, Canberra, Australia, 16 February 1987, pp. S00798–S00810.

Tisdell, C. A. (1988a). "Economic impact of biological control of weeds and insects." Newcastle, New South Wales, Australia: University of Newcastle, 2308, mimeo; paper presented to XVIII Congress of Entomology, Vancouver.

Tisdell, C. A. (1988b). "Sustainable development: Differing perspectives of ecologists and economists and relevance to LDCs." *World Development*, 16 (3): 373–384.

Tisdell, C. A. (19889). "Economic impact of biological control weeds and insects." In M. Mackaver, L. E. Ehler, and J. Roland (Eds.), *Critical Issues in Biological Control* (pp. 301–316). Andover, Hants, U.K.: Intercept.

Tisdell, C. A., and Alauddin, M. (1988). "Diversification and stability implications of new crop varieties: Theoretical and empirical evidence." Newcastle, New South Wales, Australia, University of Newcastle, mimeo; paper presented at Australian Agricultural Economics Conference, La Trobe University, February 1988.

Tisdell, C. A., Auld, B. A., and Menz, K. M. (1984). "On assessing the value of biological control of weeds." *Protection Ecology*, 6: 169–179.

Tisdell, C. A., and Fairbairn, I. J. (1983). "Development problems and planning in a resource-poor Pacific country: The case of Tuvalu." *Public Administration and Development*, 3: 341–359.

Tisdell, C. A., and Fairbairn, I. J. (1984). "Subsistence economies and unsustainable development and trade: Some simple theory." *Journal of Development Studies*, 20: 227–241.

Tisdell, C. A., and Fairbairn, T. I. (1984). "Labour supply constraints on industrialization and production deficiencies in traditional sharing societies." *Journal of Economic Development*, 9 (2): 7–33.

Todaro, M. P. (1969). "A model of labor migration and urban unemployment in less developed countries." *The American Economic Review*, 59: 138–148.

Todaro, M. P. (1971). "Income expectations, rural–urban migration and employment in Africa." *International Labor Review*, 104: 387–413.

van den Bosch, R., and Messenger, P. S. (1973). *Biological Control*. New York: Intext Educational Publishers.

van Wijnbergen, S. (1984). "The Dutch disease: A disease after all?" *Economic Journal*, 94: 41–55.

Vernon, A. (1988). "Hoiho—hermit of penguins." *The Southland Times*, Part 1 (3 March), p. 30; Part 2 (6 April), p. 28; Part 3 (13 April), p. 26.

Ward, R. G. (1982). *Australia Since the Coming of Man*. Sydney, Australia: Landsdowne Press.

Ward, R. G. (1986). "Workshop on Pacific islands—Australian issues." Academy of Social Sciences in Australia, mimeo.

Walsh, R. G., Loomis, J. B., and Gillman, R. A. (1984). "Valuing option, existence and bequest demands for wilderness." *Land Economics*, 60: 14–29.

Weisbrod, B. (1964). "Collective-consumption services of individual-consumption goods." *Quarterly Journal of Economics*, 78: 471–477.

Western, D. (1982). "Amboseli National Park: Enlisting landowners to conserve migratory wildlife." *Ambio*, 11 (5): 302–308.

Wilson, F., and Huffaker, C. B. (1976). "The philosophy, scope and importance of biological control." In C. B. Huffaker and P. S. Messenger (Eds.), *Theory and Practice of Biological Control*, (pp. 3–15). New York: Academic Press.

Wise, W. S. (1978). "The economic analysis of agricultural research." *Research and Development Management*, 8: 185–189.

World Commission on Environment and Development (1987). *Our Common Future*. Oxford, U.K.: Oxford University Press.

Worster, D. (1985). *Nature's Economy: A History of Ecological Ideas*. Cambridge, U.K.: Cambridge University Press.

Yellow-eyed Penguin Trust (1987). "Yellow-eyed Penguin: Information Sheet." Yellow-eyed Penguin Trust, P. O. Box 5409, Dunedin, N.Z., mimeo.

Yellow-Eyed Penguin Trust (1988). "A threatened species, research findings, objectives." Yellow-eyed Penguin Trust, P. O. Box 5409, Dunedin, N.Z., mimeo.

Yotopolous, P. A., and Nugent, J. B. (1976). *Economics of Development*. New York: Harper & Row.

Index

land, 17, 25, 32; ethnic, 22; values,
  variation as a measure of
  benefit of pest control, 110, 111
law and order, and conservation,
  53
Lecomber, R., 4, 57, 63, 66, 69
Leibenstein, H., 28, 34, 35
Leopold, A., 21
less developed countries, 34, 35;
  conservation, 39; and
  urbanization, 17
Lewis, W. A., 9, 118, 119, 127,
  128, 132
Liew, J., 147
limits to growth, 57–72
Little, I. M. D., 55, 118
little blue penguin, 94, 95; as a
  tourist attraction, 95, 96
Loomis, J. B., 152
low-level equilibrium-trap, 34, 35

Madagascar, 15
Maitra, P., 35, 57, 71, 121, 149,
  150
Malthus, T. R., 17, 25, 30, 31, 37
Malthusians, 25, 26
Mamo, 15
managers, and the environment,
  14
Mandel, E., 149
mangroves, 56
manufacturing: and development
  of LDCs, 118; returns in,
  compared to agriculture in
  LDCs, 122; sector, in LDCs,
  127
Mao, Y., 130
Maoris, 15, 41, 42
marine areas, 55
market: bias, 44; system [and
  conservation, 6, 15; and
  conservation in LDCs, 43, 44,

  45; and environmental concern,
  12, 13]
Marris, R., 14, 47
Marsden, J., 103
Marshall, A., 142
Marshallian case, increasing then
  decreasing returns, 142–46
Martel, L., 65, 66
Marx, K., 31
Marxists, 29
McArthur, A. T. G., 85
Meadows, D. L., 57, 58, 62
Means, G. C., 46, 166
Megadyptes antipodes, 90
Meier, G. M., 29, 121, 127
Mellor, J. W., 142
Mellor's case, constant returns,
  142
Mentis, M. T., 22
Menz, K., 102, 104, 111
Messenger, P.S., 102
Micronesia, and United States,
  138
migration: international, 9 [from
  developing countries, 136–54;
  and per capita income, 138;
  and poverty in LDCs, 157];
  permanent versus temporary,
  154; profile, 140; rural–urban,
  117; urban–rural, 9
migratory, species and
  conservation, 49
minimax: loss, 82; loss, and
  species preservation, 79, 80;
  regret, 82; regret, and species
  preservation, 80, 81
MIRAB economies, 136, 137
MIRAG economies, 136
Mirrlees, J. A., 55
Mishan, E. J., 36
Mishra, H. R., 54
moa, 15

About the Author

CLEMENT A. TISDELL is Professor of Economics at the University of Queensland, Australia, and the author of numerous books and articles on economic development and environmental subjects.